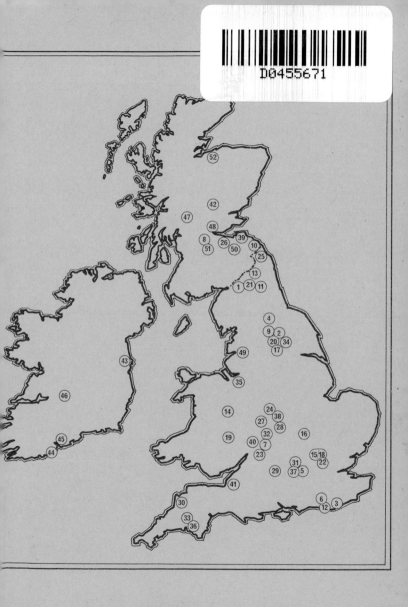

Guide to the Battlefields
of Britain and Ireland

Guide to the Battlefields of Britain and Ireland

Lt Col Howard Green, MC, FSA

Constable London

First published in Great Britain 1973
by Constable and Company Ltd
10 Orange Street, London WC2H 7EG
Copyright © 1973 by Lieutenant-Colonel Howard Green

ISBN 0 09 459280 2

Set in 'Monotype' Ehrhardt
Printed in Great Britain
by W & J Mackay Limited, Chatham

For Katrina, Camilla and Clare
with my love

Contents

Illustrations

Acknowledgements

The author gratefully records the help he received from: the Reverend J. W. Mansell, vicar of Naseby; the vicar of Long Marston (for Marston Moor); Mr and Mrs Evans, of 'Battlefield' (for Shrewsbury); the Reverend Canon Miles Brown, of St Winnow (for both Lostwithiel battles); Mr Hill-Wood, of Urrard House, Killiecrankie; Miss Venning, of Bude (for Stratton); Miss Fairweather, of Glencoe; Mr Parkinson, of Chadbury (for Evesham); Mr Peter Kerr-Dinneen for Rottingdean; Miss Skipsy, of Shaw House School, Newbury; Mr Rankin, of Branxton (for Flodden); Major-General A. MacLennan, OBE, late RAMC (for Sheriff-muir); the Reverend E. R. Boston, vicar of Sutton Cheney, Mrs Wright, of Ambion Hill Farm (for Bosworth); and Major A. W. Wyncoll (for Otterburn).

Permission to reproduce the illustrations was granted by the following: page 18 (W. A. Poucher, FRPS), pages 28, 267 (J. Allan Cash Ltd), pages 50, 109, 135, 151, 201, 256 and 284 (Radio Times Hulton Picture Library). All the remaining illustrations are reproduced from photographs taken by the author. The maps were drawn by Patrick Leeson.

Introduction

This book is an endeavour to escort the reader across those battlefields, some famous, others almost unknown, on which his ancestors may have fought and made history. It is intended for two types of people. Firstly, it is for the motoring historian to keep in his car. On passing a signpost pointing to 'Naseby', 'Glencoe', 'Mortimer's Cross' or 'Kinsale' he may turn aside, refer to the relevant chapter and there get an outline account of the battle and what he may expect to find on the site. With him may be a companion, studying the map. Seeing the non-committal symbol of crossed swords and a date may arouse a curiosity which this book is intended to satisfy.

The other reader is the more serious historian, whose appetite may be whetted by what he reads in this book. He already knows a good deal about Hastings, Tewkesbury, Culloden, Barnet and the Boyne and may wish to 'see for himself' on the field with a map and a photograph what he has learned in the study. This book may help him.

One of the great tragedies of our history has been the large number of bloody battles fought in the British Isles between our own peoples. The only exceptions are Hastings and Stamford Bridge. The vast majority of them were between parties of Englishmen separated only by political differences, differences arising from each man's conviction that he should support either the monarch on his throne, acclaimed and lawfully crowned, or alternatively the will of the people, democracy.

On arrival at any battlefield the visitor will be told – 'Oh, there is nothing to be seen here now.' This is quite wrong. There is always something to be seen, even if it is only the side of a hill down which an enemy charged, as at Flodden, or a river over which a vital bridge was fought for, as at Boroughbridge, or a hedgerow between two fields, as at Towton. There is always something to be seen.

As I went round the four countries of the British Isles visiting the battlefields I was struck by the frequency with which a river, stream or marsh greatly influenced so many of the actions. Other physical features such as woods, roads, buildings, steep hills, occasionally were of importance but their influence, even combined, barely equalled that of rivers or water.

Perhaps this book may demonstrate the importance of these natural features. Although the armies and troops engaged have long since passed away, these natural features have not. They are still there, ready to be examined and considered: they offer a silent welcome to the interested historian.

I make no apology for including in this book Hadrian's Wall, which was the scene of constant fighting, if not of a single famous battle; nor Glencoe, with its enduring sinister atmosphere, and Runnymede, so far-reaching in its effect. In neither case was a battle fought there but they are so notorious and so easily found and inspected that they are well worth a visit.

Howard Green

Craigwell Manor, Aldwick, 1973

Hadrian's Wall (AD 125)

About AD 120 the Roman invasion of the British Isles reached its limit along what became the border from Carlisle to Newcastle. Beyond this line the Romans found a mountainous country, far less productive than England, which was already being colonized by Roman efficiency. The Scots resisted the Romans valiantly and with such success that the Romans felt the game was not worth the candle – the price was too high, the prize too meagre.

Accordingly, they discontinued their probing raids and withdrew to the narrowest, and therefore the most easily defensible, neck of land between the two larger areas – namely the border. Knowing the warlike and almost savage qualities of the Scots, the Romans built a great wall to keep the Scots out of England and to deter them from raiding. The wall, a great military fortification, was garrisoned by Roman troops frequently at full strength. The wall was started in AD 122 and took 8 years to build. It is 73 miles long and runs from Wallsend to the east of Newcastle, westward to the Solway Firth. For most of the way the road B6318 runs close beside it, sometimes on the north side of the wall and later on the southern.

Tactically it is excellently sited, and usually runs along the top of high ground. An attacker, 'blown' after climbing the frequently steep escarpments in front, then had to tackle the 20-foot wall. In those days scaling ladders or ropes with grappling irons were unknown and thus for 1,100 years the wall was impassable. There was a large fort every 17 miles, strongly garrisoned, while smaller 'milecastles' were built about a mile apart. A deep ditch or moat 9 feet deep ran along the north side of the wall in some places where the occasional absence of a natural rise in the ground demanded it.

The wall was 20 feet high, and at its top 8 feet thick. Behind it, and close to it for much of its length, was dug a 20-foot-wide ditch known as the *vallum*, 8 feet deep. Neither its use nor the reason for its excavation is known.

Usually the wall was garrisoned by auxiliary troops from all parts of the Empire under Roman officers, but one of the three regular Roman legions always stationed in England was on short notice at all times to march up and strengthen any threatened point. The garrison was accommodated in the forts along the wall, and there was little depth of defence. At full manning, 6,000 men were employed.

It is still a magnificent piece of military engineering. Some of the great slabs of dressed stone are 2 feet long and 1 foot deep, although the majority are 1-foot cubes. The tens of thousands needed indicate prodigious labour, not only in erecting them but in bringing them to the site. Stonehenge and the great pyramids of Egypt include much greater stones, but in these cases the building materials were needed at only one comparatively small site where the whole architectural construction was under the immediate eye of the director of operations. But the construction of Hadrian's Wall was of necessity under several, perhaps ten or more, subordinate planners, and they again had lesser sub-controllers under them. It is estimated that the workforce required to open the quarries, dig the wells, build the storehouses behind the line and finally to build the wall itself was not less than 20,000, mostly local labour. It was a work of far-sighted imagination and reflects the Roman genius for organization.

Very broadly there were three separate tactical areas for the wall. On the right, facing the Scots, cavalry were intended to be used. The terrain to the north of the wall here is open Northumbrian plain with moorland grass. Slopes are easy, and although there were certain areas of forest in the first century, it made ideal cavalry country. Consequently, the exits through the wall at the major forts were wide enough to permit large bodies of horsemen to emerge at speed, while each party was within reasonable distance of the next when the wall had been cleared.

The middle section of the wall was built for infantry. The ground beyond the escarpment was unsuitable for mounted men, the bogs and considerable number of loughs restricting manoeuvre. More importantly, the natural rise of the ground outside the wall is much steeper than elsewhere, making an enemy's advance more difficult and the defenders' task behind their crenellations along the top of the wall more effective.

The western third of the wall was again designed for mounted men or rather for their exits out on to the flatter moorland to the north.

As the Romans gradually colonized England through the second and third centuries, they replaced the men in the ranks of the army with Englishmen and the military situation was very similar to that in India, prior to about 1930. The framework and senior officers of units were of the paramount ruling power while the junior officers, NCOs and men in the ranks were volunteers enlisted from the local population. By 415, however, when the Romans finally left England, the wall was entirely garrisoned by Englishmen against the Scotsmen, who naturally believed that the English were trying to fence them in.

Today, for some miles to the west of Chollerford, the wall is 8 feet high in many places. It is possible, at certain places marked by signboards, to climb and walk along it. The footway along the top is now grass-grown and the walking is easy. It is still possible to see some of the battlements with their embrasures. The bigger forts are easily seen and, although

now in ruins, they give a good idea of the size of the rooms
and the stone stairs within the buildings. Good examples are
at Housesteads and Steel Rig. There are frequent small car
parks.

Naturally there have been depredations of some of the
great stones and the walls between the modern fields out in
front obviously include many of them. But large sections are
exactly as they were when built in AD 125 and inspection in
the field shows how meticulously they were originally laid.
It is surprising that nature has made little use of the chinks
between the stones for parasite weed-growths. Except for

Hadrian's Wall near Housesteads

turf on the top, most of the wall is entirely bare.

On a clear day the view from the higher stretches of the wall is magnificent. Near Greenhead one can see far into Dumfriesshire to the north-west, while a similar view is obtained of the Cheviots to the north-east. One can be sure that the views seen today are precisely those the Romans saw 1,800 years ago.

The wall ran where Newcastle stands today, one of the bigger forts being in the centre of today's city. The wall followed, approximately, the line of Gallowgate, Blackett Street and New Bridge Street, but there are no actual remains of the wall left in the city. However, in central Newcastle cracks in house-walls mark the line where the filling of the outer ditch and the *vallum* has caused the ground to subside fractionally under the weight of the nineteenth century.

Hadrian's Wall is easier to explore and to understand than any other Roman remains in the world, the Colosseum in Rome included. It is a magnificent monument to one of the greatest nations history has seen.

Alongside the fort at Brocolitia and about 100 yards below it lies the perfect little temple of Mithras. It has recently been excavated and is in a remarkably good condition for its 1,700 years.

Stamford Bridge (1066)

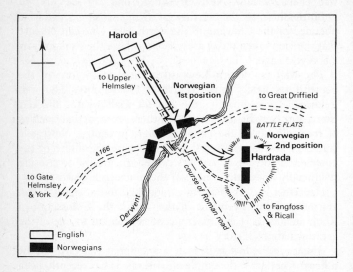

Every Englishman and woman has heard of the Battle of Hastings, the greatest turning-point in British history. Very few know anything about an important engagement fought only three weeks previously in Yorkshire, the Battle of Stamford Bridge, when for the first time in our history a foreign invader was defeated and thrown from our shores.

Harold's younger brother Tostig, Earl of Northumbria, had made himself so unpopular with his people that he abdicated and retired to Norway. Disgruntled, he joined the King of Norway, Harold Hardrada.

During the summer William the Conqueror was assembling an army and ships along the coast of Normandy for one of the greatest expeditions in history. Harold had his army along the coasts of Sussex and Kent watching and waiting. Nothing happened, and the men got bored and began to disperse.

Suddenly Tostig and Hardrada landed with 6,000 men from 300 ships on the coast of Yorkshire, sailing up the Humber. They disembarked and moving to the vicinity of York defeated a scratch force at Fulford, on the present golf-course. Then instead of taking the old Roman city the invaders withdrew to their ships in the river Ouse at Riccall 8 miles away.

Hearing of the Norwegian invasion, Harold had no alternative but to leave unguarded the south coast and march north to meet the Norsemen – and his brother. Many of the bored soldiers, hearing of the prospect of repelling an invader, rejoined and a great march of 250 miles followed.

On 25 September Harold arrived in York, and hearing that the invaders were resting at Stamford, 8 miles away on the river Derwent, marched at once to attack them. Harold had 4,000 men to meet Hardrada's 5,000. (1,000 had been left on the ships at Riccall.)

The enemy held a position by the old mill, covering a narrow footbridge over the river about 300 yards upstream from the present road-bridge at Stamford Bridge and just below the present weir. Their line about 100 yards north of the river was on a frontage of 300 yards. On the south side of the river their second line stood 200 yards back from the little bridge. The bridge, the only link between the two portions of the force, was very narrow, allowing only one man at a time to cross. Because its only link consisted of this narrow bridge the whole enemy position was bad.

Harold marched up what is now the A166 through Gate Helmsley and deployed his force just short of the present caravan site on the north bank, his right group astride this road.

Harold charged the enemy front line and drove it down to

the river, a success largely due to surprise, the Norwegians having no idea the English were so near. Hardrada gave the order to cross the bridge and take up a new position on the south side, farther back. There is a legend that the bridge was held by a giant Norseman with a great battle-axe for half an hour, while his fleeing companions escaped under his arm and its flailing axe. Eventually he fell wounded as the last man crossed and Harold led his army across.

Taking up a position opposite Hardrada's newly formed line, held by a continuous row of shields, the English again advanced and both sides were locked in combat. The ground where this fight took place is on Battle Flats, a level piece of ground 50 feet above the river and 200 yards east of the little bridge. Hardrada was wounded and Tostig, now in command, was offered his life if his forces withdrew. But hoping that the 1,000 men left on the ships at Riccall would arrive as reinforcements, he refused to surrender or withdraw. On their arrival these new men, exhausted by their forced march in heavy armour on a bad road, were quickly liquidated by Harold, who then renewed his attack. Only a few survivors reached their boats on the Ouse. Of the 300 ships used in the landing only 24 were needed for re-embarkation.

That night, while feasting in York to celebrate his victory, Harold heard that William of Normandy had landed at Pevensey. At once he marched his army back to the south, and by a stupendous effort covered in 12 days almost 260 miles, to fight the Battle of Hastings.

There is still something to be seen at Stamford Bridge battle-field today. The site of the old bridge can be accurately pin-pointed, the weir nearby giving a precise indication of its position, and the rocks undoubtedly carried the wooden piers- Alongside the last house overlooking the river (Mr Long.

bottom's garage) is about 20 yards of 'promenade' 10 feet above the water. From it the river, the site of the little bridge, the weir and the present caravan site can be seen, all within 200 yards. On the minute little village green 50 yards back from the bridge is a rough-hewn memorial stone with inscriptions in English and Norwegian. The top edge of the slope up to Battle Flats on the road to Barmby-on-the-Moor is now covered by houses, but behind their gardens lies the flat ground on which Hardrada formed his line of shields.

Hastings (1066)

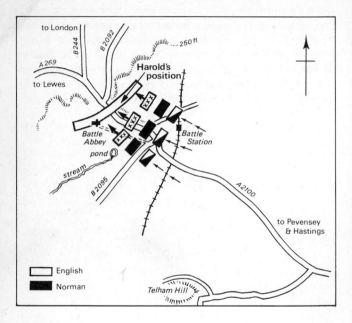

Hastings is easily the most important battle ever fought by the British. The chief result of our defeat was to unite the petty kingdoms of Wessex, East Anglia, Mercia and Northumbria under one strong government in London, whereby the monarch ruled by near-dictatorship.

When Edward the Confessor died in 1066, Harold, Earl of Wessex, already nominated by Edward as his successor, was hurriedly placed on the throne by the nobles and crowned, to prevent other candidates pushing their claims and possibly setting off a civil war.

In 1061 Duke William of Normandy, when on a state visit to England, had also been promised the succession to the English crown, and clearly on the Confessor's death trouble was likely. Harold had no blood claim to the throne, only his election by the nobles. William of Normandy had a far better claim, his great-grandmother, Emma, having been married to the Confessor's father.

On hearing of Harold's coronation Duke William, not unjustifiably, felt affronted and determined to assert his claim to England's crown. He decided to invade and throughout the spring and summer of 1066 built ships, collected men and stores, commandeered horses, and prepared his 'D' Day.

Harold, knowing of these preparations, collected an army in Kent and Sussex, but hearing of the Norwegian invasion of York in September left the south coast and marched north to meet the more immediate threat. On the very night of his victory at the Battle of Stamford Bridge he heard of William's landing at Pevensey, near Hastings. He immediately marched south, the army covering nearly 400 miles in 29 days in its two forced marches, a phenomenal effort, the main roads (i.e. the only roads) being little more than cart-tracks. The men's footwear was made of felt and they had to 'find' their own food each night.

Meanwhile William on landing had been prudence personified. He built a stockade with prefabricated materials brought over from Normandy, landed his stores and dragged his ships up the beach. Here their masts were unstepped and they lay within the bridgehead safe from attack by sea from the Thames.

On 13 October William heard of the advance of Harold's force through the Weald of Kent, and on 14 October he advanced towards London and prepared for a head-on collision. As he passed through Telham he heard that an army was drawn up along a ridge 2 miles away. Immediately he halted for his 3-mile column to close up, and then deployed approximately along the line of the modern railway from Tunbridge Wells to Hastings, while he galloped on to observe Harold's position. It covered 800 yards, its left being across the modern A2100, while the right was opposite a small hillock, 200 yards out in front. The slope that fell away in front was, and is, parkland, with good turf and only the occasional tree.

Along the whole front was a continuous line of infantrymen, shoulder to shoulder, who with their shields held in front formed an imposing line. Armed with double-handed axes they stood in alternate groups with the few archers available. In the front line were the 'house-carls' or regulars, and behind them the men collected on the forced march from Stamford Bridge. These had little or no training and were armed only with spears, stone-headed clubs or pitchforks.

The Normans took up a position on the downward, northern slope of Telham Hill, about 400 yards from the English and on a line parallel to, and exactly covering off, their opponents. There they halted, in full view, a rehearsal for Waterloo.

The Norman archers advanced, the crossbowmen moving up to the hillock, where they discharged a torrent of arrows. Effective at first, because the scarcity of English archers precluded an adequate reply, the ammunition ran out, and the infantry had to advance uphill to attack the shield-wall, which had very few gaps in it. On the Norman left the Bretons, on reaching the English line, met such a murderous reception that they turned and fled.

The exultant English right flank now lost its head, disobeyed Harold's strict orders not to break ranks or move forward except at his signal and followed the fleeing Bretons downhill and round the hillock. The main Norman line, seeing the retreat on their left, began to waver. Their arrows exhausted, the English wall unbroken, they began to drift back.

Now leadership played its part. Duke William removed his helmet so that all could see him and dashing into the midst of the fugitives used his powerful voice and imperious manner to stop the retreat. He then launched his cavalry from behind the centre of his line forward and, wheeling left, directed them against the pursuing English in the valley below the hillock.

These advancing English were overwhelmed, few getting back to their original line. A pause ensued, luckily for William. Half his army was disorganized, with one section defeated, and clearly a new plan had to be made. Harold, too, was glad of a brief respite so that he could fill the gap caused by the impetuous right flank, dress his line, be seen by his men and generally grip the situation. The pause probably lasted an hour, both sides calling for more arrows.

About midday William launched his 'Old Guard', his precious cavalry, against the unbroken English line. Up the hill they charged. The horses, carrying the enormous weight of knights in Norman armour, were almost blown with the gigantic physical effort demanded of them. The English front-line regulars wielding their two-handed axes did great execution against the horses, and the noise of clashing weapons and armour, shouting by men on either side and the breathless snorting of the horses must have been deafening. The Normans lost heavily, and they finally withdrew, many in despair at their impossible task.

Again some of the English disobeyed orders and, breaking ranks, followed the retreating cavalry down the hill into the valley between the two lines. Here some fresh enemy cavalry charged them and of course cut them to pieces.

William now made a combined offensive. His archers advanced slightly and used plunging-fire on the rearward

Senlac Hill site of the battle of Hastings

English lines, while under this covering fire some uncommitted cavalry charged the front line, which as a result of the
first great charge had many gaps. Following the horsemen,
the Norman infantry broke through the dissolving line, while
the English irregulars called up to fill the spaces broke and
fled. The situation was becoming desperate when tragedy
supervened. Harold was struck in the eye; although in great
pain, he managed to keep standing. But the word spread that
he was killed. The regulars closed their ranks round their
king, the Normans closing in.

Eventually, as dusk was falling, a party of Norman knights
hacked their way into the rapidly diminishing circle where,
finding Harold supported by some servants, they killed him.
The line disintegrated, the men turning into the forest behind
them. William remained on the field victorious, the King of
England to be.

Coming up from Hastings on the A2100 the visitor should
turn left just beyond the Senlac Hotel (on the right) into
Powdermill Lane. This second-class road runs just behind the
Norman first position. At the corner of the lane is the lodge
gate of Battle Abbey Park, near where the arrow that wounded
Harold was fired. Five hundred yards farther on down the
lane is the best viewpoint of the whole battle. Immediately on
the right of the road is a string of fish ponds. They did not
exist in 1066 and were dug to drain the marsh in the low
ground and take the stream running down from near the
lodge gates. The Bretons who made the first attack, advanced
between the biggest pond – the size of a football field – and
the next one higher up the little valley. The hillock in front
of the English line is clear but not impressive, but the slope
up which the Bretons had to charge is steeper than I expected.
If William, instead of crossing this marsh and then climbing

the steep rise, as he did on the left, had attacked on the right, he would have had a much easier path to follow, and in addition have threatened Harold's vulnerable left flank. But, of course, he had had little time for reconnaissance.

From this viewpoint 500 yards west from the lodge gates, along Powdermill Lane, this tactical solution is very apparent. William, although he won probably the most decisive victory in history, was not such a great general as is believed, although a great leader.

The second viewpoint not to be missed is the terrace of Battle Abbey girls' school, admission to which is obtainable down a lane running off from the main car park outside the abbey gateway. The English line ran immediately in front of the terrace and its extent to the west and the important hillock can be seen. To the east, trees and buildings conceal the view. To the front the view overlooking the fish ponds, Powdermill Lane, Telham Hill and the whole of the western half of the battlefield is superb. In the inner gardens of the school, which can be reached from the terrace, is the spot where Harold fell. Here a monument, the Norman Stone, has been erected on the site of the high altar of the abbey built by William the Conqueror. Vestiges of the Norman abbey can still be seen, although it was largely rebuilt in the fifteenth century. Around this stone a party of Norman and Breton historians hold a memorial service every October. In 1966, Queen Elizabeth II, the twenty-ninth monarch in descent from the Conqueror, stood on this terrace surveying the scene of the most important battle in our history, while the President of the Historical Society gave her and the Duke of Edinburgh a short account of the action.

The Standard (1138)

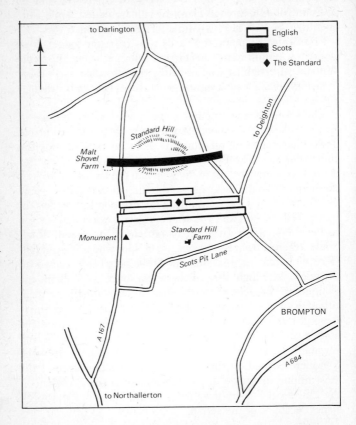

Henry I died in 1135. He had only one surviving legitimate child, the Empress Matilda, married to a German prince. She clearly had the best possible claim to the throne of

England, but in those days it was unthinkable for the monarch to be a woman and many of the barons would not accept her. Her cousin, Stephen of Blois, also a grandchild of William the Conqueror, was accordingly invited to come over from Normandy and assume the crown. He was well liked, 31 years old and showed great promise. His reign, however, was marred by constant squabbles and rebellions about his claim to the throne, far inferior to that of Matilda. She was an able, strong-minded woman and naturally tried to claim her undoubted rights, in spite of her sex. She had been promised help by King David I of Scotland who, having claims on parts of Northumberland himself, decided to invade England, ostensibly on her behalf. He crossed the frontier at Carlisle and, marching over the Pennines via Penrith and Brough, reached Darlington with an army of about 12,000. Under his command were a few archers, some pony-mounted cavalry and a large body of wild Galloway Picts.

King Stephen dispatched an army up from the south under the command of Thurston, Archbishop of York. Many recruits flocked to his enormous standard, which in fact was a ship's mast topped by a small vessel containing wafers consecrated for Holy Communion. It was carried on a great farm cart and was regarded by the men in the ranks with the same reverence and respect as were the regimental colours of regiments several centuries later.

The two forces met on Cowton Moor, 3 miles north of Northallerton, just over a mile north-west of the village of Brompton (on the A684).

The English took up a position in depth with the archers in front, the spearmen behind them, and the mounted men forming a third line. The standard erected on its great cart was posted in the middle of the second line. The army occupied a frontage of 800 yards, and was about 200 yards from front to rear. Standard Hill Farm (which belongs today to Mrs Jameson) stands approximately in the position of the rearmost English line.

The Scots formed up in line facing the English, with King David's group on the left, the great mass of the Galloway Picts in the centre and young Prince Henry, son of King David, on the right with the cavalry. Their right was by the present Malt Shovel Farm and their centre where the northern Standard Hill Farm (belonging to Mr Johnson) stands today. Both positions are tactically sound.

The Picts started the battle by a wild rush against the English archers, who checked them. The well-disciplined spearmen then took over the line from the archers, who with-

The Scottish position before their advance. Their right was by the Malt Shovel Farm, the white house in the left centre, their centre to the right of the buildings in the right centre

drew to replenish their quivers, and the English remained a steady, solid, unbroken phalanx of men.

Prince Henry, seeing the repulse of the Picts, then led his horsemen forward, round the English left wing, to attack the rearward services, the baggage wagons and the led horses. However, the archbishop loosed his third line, his cavalry, which wheeled round to its left and charged the young prince. A mighty struggle took place round what are now Mrs Jameson's farmhouse and buildings, and slightly to its rear toward Scots Pit Lane, with the most fearful chaos. Individual combats were universal, bloody and hate-ridden. Eventually the English overcame the Scots cavalry, though the Danes and

Normans in the Scots army fought on valiantly for a while; but eventually they too gave up, and the whole invading army collapsed. In the utter confusion just before the end, King David and Prince Henry escaped from the field, their absence not being noticed.

Ten thousand men from the two armies were killed and are buried in Scots Pits Lane, a broad heavily wooded glade, 300 yards behind Standard Hill Farm South. Running east–west, from the main Northallerton–Darlington Road (A167) to the lesser road from Brompton, it is easily found. Less than a century ago some bones and pieces of metal accoutrements were uncovered in the hedge lining the glade, where they had lain for 800 years.

A monument to the battle stands on the A167, and is easily found. Imaginatively, it was erected precisely where the left of the English third line was posted.

Runnymede (1215)

In the history of the world there have been several pieces of parchment that have changed the course of history. America's Declaration of Independence of 1776 was perhaps the most far-reaching. The treaty declaring the neutrality of Belgium guaranteed by the Great Powers in 1830 was blatantly ignored in 1914 by Germany, the Kaiser sneeringly referring to it as 'a scrap of paper'. The revocation of the Edict of Nantes by Louis XIV in 1685 not only caused many Protestants to lose their lives but drove many out of France into Holland and thence, with the Dutch colonists, to South Africa, bringing with them elements of culture and refinement. In this century the German–Russian Treaty of Non-Aggression of 1939 – to be torn up at Hitler's whim in 1941 – and the Treaty of Rome setting up the Common Market both had and will have a vast impact on history.

But none has so directly influenced the ordinary Englishman as the signing of Magna Carta, forced upon King John in 1215.

Prior to the Norman Conquest England had consisted of four powerful sub-kingdoms – Mercia, Northumbria, East Anglia and Wessex. Frequently they were at loggerheads with each other, and always subject to raids by Danes and Saxons. Life was chaotic, there was no organized defence, no common currency, few laws common to each kingdom and a general feeling of insecurity.

The Conquest changed all that. William united the four sub-kingdoms and ruled from Westminster with a hard but efficient near-dictatorship.

During the 130 years following the Conquest the English absorbed the Normans, the Saxons and the Danes. There were no more raids and the people grew together into one nation, but with much mixed blood. Three strong kings had accustomed the people to the strong rule and undoubtedly the English were grateful to the Normans for setting up the new pattern of life. They felt secure, and the great families still held great power. Many of them were the descendants of the original Norman knights and felt naturally loyal to the monarch.

In 1199 Richard I died with no legitimate offspring and his brother John succeeded him. At once he ruled harshly and not for the benefit of his country. He quarrelled with the Church, refusing to accept the Pope's nominee as archbishop; he lost most of England's territories in France; he enforced extortionate taxation on the people against the advice of the Great Council; and he openly and frequently punished, and often executed, malefactors without trial.

The articulate elements of society, clerical, noble and lay, eventually and by the sheer power of public opinion forced him to sign the Great Charter, Magna Carta.

Knowing what was afoot, John had imported mercenaries to resist. He implored the support of the Pope, he offered to go on a crusade to the Holy Land and tried to wriggle out of signing. But the barons were too strong for him. His friends, already very lukewarm, deserted him at Runnymede, an island in the Thames, and on 15 June 1215 he reluctantly signed.

Why was the charter so important to the British people? Out of the sixty-three clauses, three have been a lasting part of the British Constitution. They are:

1 No taxation by the Crown, only by Parliament.
2 The Church to elect its own leaders, appointments which the Crown must accept.
3 No man to be tried except by a court of law.

These three great principles are today, and have been, since their independence, in the USA, the very essence of democracy, and the basis of our liberties.

Four copies of the charter were made, two of which are in the British Museum, one being on view. Lincoln and Salisbury cathedrals each have a copy.

Today the A308 from Windsor to Staines crosses Runnymede Meadows. They are a mile long, 300 yards wide, and the road runs very close to the river Thames. About half way along them the so-called Magna Carta Islet can be seen alongside the north bank.

Traditionally this little slip of land, only 200 yards by 40 yards, is the site of the great signing. But, surrounded by the deep, fast-flowing river, difficult of access and limited in space, it seems a most improbable place to choose for a confrontation so momentous as this was obviously going to be. Both King John and the barons were attended by a large retinue and there is insufficient room for the great medieval marquees with which the great always travelled. There is no indication that the river has changed its course, making the islet smaller today than it was in 1215. Both banks are sheer and firm and after heavy rain the water is 4 feet below the meadow level.

There was nothing to be gained by transporting numbers of men across this very considerable water obstacle in primitive river boats, when the extensive Runnymede Meadow, from which they would have embarked, is available nearby, spacious and with a road (or in 1215 no doubt a track) leading up to it.

Lastly, the concluding words of the Great Charter are: 'Given under our hand on the meadow of Runnymede, 15th June, 1215'. No hint of any island here and perhaps legend and tradition have been mistaken in always maintaining that the charter was signed on the island. It is highly unlikely.

Opposite the islet and across the meadow on its southern side, on a slight rise, is the Magna Carta memorial, a small, attractive little belvedere, erected by the American Law Association. From its slight eminence the whole of the wide sweep of Runnymede Meadow can be seen and there is a strong probability that, as the visitor walks from the road across the football pitches to the memorial, he is passing over land on which King John walked, and signed.

Farther to the west and up a considerable slope, but with a good and easy path, lies the John F. Kennedy memorial. A magnificent piece of carved granite, it too surveys the important meadow below it.

Lewes (1264)

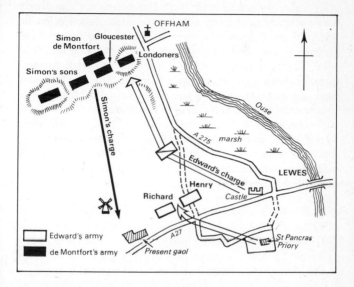

The greatest political event in English history is Magna Carta, wrung from King John by the barons in 1215. John's son and successor, Henry III, believing in the divine right of kings, gradually eroded the clauses and principles of the charter and by 1255 England was once again under a dictatorship. Henry was not even an efficient dictator.

Simon de Montfort, a brilliant, able, very religious Frenchman, had settled in England. Being well-born, he reached the court, married the king's sister and quickly became Henry's chief adviser. But after a while he rebelled against the growing dictatorial methods of his brother-in-law and the frequent and often blatant repudiations of the charter. Accordingly he joined sides with the barons to restore such democracy as the Great Charter had created.

By 1260, so exasperated were the barons by the king's whole attitude to the law that they unanimously elected de Montfort to lead them against the throne, to support the rights of the people and to declare war on the king.

In May 1264 Simon de Montfort marched from London to Lewes with 5,000 men, there to meet Henry. The king's army was almost twice the size of Simon's, and his second-in-command was his son Edward, a brilliant young man, who was to become one of England's greatest kings, the 'Hammer of the Scots', and the father of the first Prince of Wales.

The baronial army reached the Downs above Lewes and took up a position along the highest ground in the vicinity, overlooking the town. One 'group', the Londoners, were posted on the left of the line and occupied a hillock just to the west of the present Lewes–London road, opposite the village of Offham. (The village has a twelfth-century church, large portions of which, standing today, were in existence in 1264.)

In the centre of the line, where a very slight dip in the ridge is just discernible, stood the Earl of Gloucester's 'group' – while Simon's two sons, Henry and Guy, jointly commanded the right wing astride the upper end of the present training gallop behind the grandstand of the 1972 Lewes racecourse. Simon kept his fourth group, mostly cavalry, in hand behind the right wing.

On the alarm being given the king's infantry, quartered in St Pancras Priory (still standing), turned out. After considerable confusion, uncertainty, counter-orders and delay it moved out of the town, taking up a position on the high ground just north of the present jail, where a new housing estate has recently been built.

Prince Edward, commanding the cavalry, was in Lewes Castle with many of his horses tethered in the High Street.

He climbed up the tower of the castle and from there saw the baronial army drawn up less than a mile away. At once he mounted his men and led them out on to the Downs and then charged Simon's left wing, the Londoners. These latter, being ill-trained and ill-disciplined, turned and ran, some reaching Croydon the following day. Edward foolishly followed them for a long way, doing great execution, but for over two hours his efficient and successful mounted force was off the field, having no influence on the action.

His rash, uncontrolled escapade was to be repeated 381 years later, at Naseby, when Prince Rupert, after a similar highly successful mounted attack, went on to plunder Cromwell's wagons and thus to deny the Royalist army the great asset of cavalry.

Simon, seeing Edward's cavalry disappearing in the distance, advanced his two remaining 'groups' down the half-mile slope to engage Henry's infantry. They met in a head-on collision a few hundred yards short of the present jail. A confused mêlée ensued, as it was to do at Evesham a year later. But at Lewes Simon had a mounted reserve which he lacked at Evesham. To settle the issue he put his mounted reserve round his right flank and cut open the king's left. The impact of his 500 cavalrymen galloping downhill on perfect turf was terrific, their impetus carrying many of the men through the royal infantry and into the streets of the town.

Prince Edward, returning from his disastrous foray, paused to plunder Simon's baggage, and in particular the baronial headquarters coach. But while doing so he saw that his father was defeated down by the town, and rode off to rejoin him at the Priory. Here they were both captured, the king to remain a baronial prisoner for more than a year. The king's brother, the ineffective Prince Richard of Cornwall, had been cut off with a handful of his men in Simon's great cavalry-flanking charge. They took refuge in a windmill but were smoked out as the battle ended. This windmill was standing until recently near the lower end of the training gallop.

The victory of the barons was a turning-point in English history. Simon de Montfort, now virtually ruling the country, determined upon democracy and summoned two locally elected burgesses from every town and two knights from every shire to London to join the Great Council of barons and bishops. The method of election was left to the local authorities concerned, who all chose the secret ballot, the embryo of our general elections today. The meeting in London of these men elected by popular vote was the beginning of our House of Commons, which has thus been in existence for over 700 years.

Coming from Brighton along the A27 the visitor, turning left at the first traffic lights, follows Nevill Road for a mile. After turning half-left up on to the Downs he will cross the training gallop, whence a short walk to the top of the ridge will give a superb view over the battlefield. This standpoint is at the extreme right flank of Simon's position. Off to the north-east along the ridge can be seen the hillock where the Londoners stood before their flight. In front is the ground down which the baronial army advanced. It is very rough downland, 500 feet up, and has never been cultivated; it is evident that all is as it was in 1264.

The southern end of the battlefield is less interesting owing to modern buildings. However about halfway along Hawkenbury Way, where it turns sharply left, a short walk across the gallop will take the visitor to the area where the windmill stood, and all round is the ground on which the mêlée took place.

Evesham (1265)

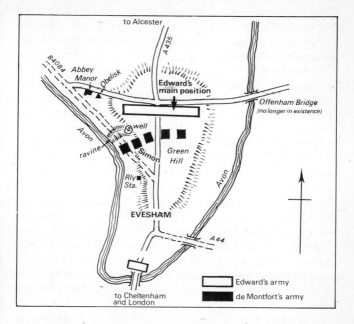

In 1216 John was succeeded by his eldest son, Henry III. He soon much incensed the barons not only by his aloof manner but also by a gradual erosion of the terms of Magna Carta. The barons had forced King John to sign it and were now exasperated to see their hard-won concessions being withdrawn.

In 1258 the barons, led by Simon de Montfort, forced the king to agree to the formation of a council of fifteen to advise, and if necessary to restrain the monarch. But soon Henry reverted to his old way of government. Five years later, in

1263, the barons appointed Simon as their leader and declared war on him and all who had supported him in his repudiation of the agreement made at Runnymede. In 1264 the two armies met at the Battle of Lewes, where Henry was captured together with his son, Prince Edward, and forced to swear his reacceptance of Magna Carta.

To strengthen his position, Simon called together a Parliament for January 1265. It was to consist of two citizens from every borough and two knights from every county, all of whom were to sit at Westminster with the barons and the bishops.

Simon de Montfort's work in setting up our House of Commons was one of the greatest events in the history of Britain, and perhaps indeed of the world.

Soon after the new Parliament had assembled, little Prince Edward, still a prisoner with his father in the hands of Simon, escaped and set up a Royalist headquarters at Worcester, where he was joined by the gentry of Shropshire and Cheshire.

At the end of July Simon's army was in and around Hereford, King Henry still with it as a prisoner of war. At Kenilworth was his young son, also Simon, just arrived from the south of England with an army slightly greater than his father's.

At Worcester, on 3 August, Edward judged correctly that Simon senior would make for Kenilworth via Evesham to join his son. He decided to march southward to prevent a junction of the two Simons and moved directly towards Evesham.

The barons under Simon de Montfort had reached the town of Evesham on the evening of 3 August. The only bridge over the Avon in 1265 stood at the south-east segment of the great loop by which the river encircles the town from the north and then veers sharply away, again northwards, enclosing Evesham in its arms.

Simon senior and his army spent the night in the town, while their enemies moved into the mouth of the peninsula.

Very early in the morning a look-out in the tower of Evesham Abbey reported troops forming up along the ridge running east and west across the main road about a mile and a half out of the town. The Royalist forces were now concentrating all along the ridge. Only a small detachment across the river continued down to the single bridge, there to block it from the east.

The frontage held by the Royalists was 2,000 yards long, and Edward had only 10,000 men. It meant only one man for every 5 yards, a very thin deployment even for a single rank in the thirteenth century. Accordingly Edward posted two very strong detachments, probably 3,000 men each, on each side of the crossroads at the top of the ridge, the Earl of Gloucester to command the right while he himself took command of the left. These 6,000 men were holding about 1,000 yards and must have been about five men to the yard, ensuring a great depth. The remaining 4,000 men were posted more thinly on the two outer flanks.

Meanwhile Simon's army was marching out of the town northward up Green Hill Road. Their departure was delayed for a while as King Henry, still their prisoner, was anxious to attend mass in the abbey and Simon, a very religious man himself, gave permission for the service to be held. The hour or so lost enabled the Royalist forces to complete their formations and to give the men a little rest, which they sorely needed.

As Simon rode up the long slope of Green Hill he could see – as he also probably knew – how both his flanks were completely blocked by the unfordable river. He could see the Royalist army motionless in its ranks along the crest of the ridge. He had recently heard that the bridge behind him, his only line of retreat, was blocked by a Royalist detachment.

He realized that a great victory or annihilation lay before him.

When about 600 yards short of the top of Green Hill the full Royalist army was seen. Along the ridge, apparently, stood an unbroken line of soldiers, several ranks deep, fierce, aggressive and presenting an unnerving sight.

At that time it was the universal practice in battle for the armies to be drawn up in lines facing each other, and then for one to advance headlong on the other. But at the sight of the menacing Royalist line Simon decided on a novel tactic. He resolved to attack in great strength the junction of the two Royalist groups about where Twyford House is today. He believed, not without reason, that he might well penetrate the line facing him.

He advanced with his cavalry, some 200 horsemen, in front. Immediately behind them he placed his prisoner, poor King Henry III, and it is difficult to find a reason for placing him there. Had he escaped and galloped forward to his own Royalist army he must have given them great encouragement and been a rallying-point in the event of disaster. Obviously such a valuable possession of the attackers would be much better out of the way, safely in the rear. Perhaps Simon wanted to be rid of his embarrassing prisoner, and deliberately put him where he could escape without great difficulty. But Simon was far too good a politician not to see how adversely Henry's escape would affect him. Putting the king in this position is one of the minor mysteries of history.

Behind the cavalry came the bulk of Simon's army. Running up from the south-west comes a ravine. With steep and deep sides in its earlier path up to the road it forms a definite obstacle to an advancing army and Gloucester commanding the Royalist right-hand group probably saw it and decided to lie up behind it.

Simon did not know of this ravine and his extreme left flank must have blundered into it just about where its head flattens out into a little marsh. As a result his left group to the west of the road tended to 'bunch' slightly to its right and cause a greater density of troops in the centre than had been intended.

Just before Simon's army reached the line of the ravine it halted briefly about 300 yards away from it. Here Simon gave his orders to his subordinate commanders and then the order to charge.

The impact of the mounted knights galloping over the almost level ground closely followed by the tightly packed body of infantry, made more dense by the bunching from the ravine, was terrific. It smashed its way into the Royalist lines, the front of which recoiled on to the rearward ones. But the latter held, and Simon's furious and excited men were immediately embroiled in heavy hand-to-hand and hand-to-horse fighting, and a more than confused mêlée developed. The noise of the clash of battle so unnerved the Welsh following up behind the English that they turned and fled.

Those uncommitted Royalist outer flanks now started to advance and wheel inwards. Edward, seeing the whole position, realized that he could by this joint inward manoeuvre entirely surround his enemy. This he succeeded in easily doing, the two outer wings meeting behind Simon and so creating a ring in which great slaughter was to take place.

It was slaughter indeed and the greater part of Simon's army was killed, or so badly wounded as to be left on the field, where they were dispatched in the evening by the Royalists.

The few who did escape got away eastward to the river down the present Blaney's Lane trying to cross the bridge at Offenham. Here they were caught and slaughtered to a man and their bodies were thrown into the river. The spot is still known as Dead Man's Ayot. The king himself was carried by the impetus of the great cavalry attack into the centre of the fighting and only saved himself by continually shouting, 'I am Harry your King. Do not kill me.' Luckily he was recognized and led off to the rear of the Royalist line, where he met his son, Prince Edward, amid great rejoicing. At some

The last fight of Simon de Montfort at Evesham

unknown time Simon was killed and by 11 am all was over. In the long run England lost. She had another 9 years of the not very effective Henry III and she lost the services of Simon de Montfort, one of the greatest politician-leaders she ever had, a statesman of the quality of William Pitt and Winston Churchill. An unseen consolation for England lay in the person of young Prince Edward, the victor of Evesham. He was a tower of strength to his father after 1265 until he himself succeeded to the throne in 1272 – to be one of England's greatest kings, and to rule for 34 years. By his personal integrity, the high tone of his private life and indeed by his imposing and regal appearance alone he raised the prestige of the Crown to a new high level.

A visit to the battlefield of Evesham is, prima facie, disappointing. Much of it is now covered with woods, orchards, a large private park with 'Keep out' notices or new houses standing in their own grounds, and perhaps less than a third can be examined. Luckily the most important area of all, where Simon made his initial great attack on the Royalist line, badly denting it, is still open and is occupied by a vast market garden.

The 'well' at the head of the ravine referred to in all accounts of the battle does not in fact exist as such, nor is it likely that it ever did. There is, however, at the ravine up from the south-west an uncharacteristic bog about the size of half a tennis-court, covered in brambles, stunted bushes, very deep grass, undergrowth and weeds. The ground is very damp and it is dangerous to penetrate very far. The bog is easily found along a cart track off to the left about 150 yards short of the crossroads at the top of Green Hill Road. Just before reaching the bog the visitor is standing in the middle of the battlefield and is within a few yards of the great mêlée.

In front, 200 yards away, about where the present orchard starts, is the position of the right flank of the Royalist right group. From here it advanced swinging left to close the trap behind Simon's army. Its right might have passed along the northern bank of the ravine and within a few yards of the visitor's position.

If the very narrow and bad cart-track, Blaney's Lane, running east from the crossroads (it is this cart-track that forms the fourth arm of the cross) is followed for 200 or 300 yards one passes out behind the rear of the housing estate, and the unexpected but pronounced declivity is seen. The track gets worse and worse but as it peters out Dead Man's Ayot can be seen across the fields.

Simon's terrible tactical blunder of crossing by the only bridge over the Avon into Evesham and thus placing himself on a tongue of land where he had little room to manoeuvre is very apparent from the map, and more so when the site is visited. Yet in the event this appallingly dangerous position had no effect on the battle whatever. Greatly superior numbers must have told, all other factors being equal.

Before leaving Evesham a visit to the great churchyard of the parish church is imperative. Herein was the old Abbey of 1265 but today its foundations have disappeared. The site of the great tower whence Nick, the Barber, saw Prince Edward's troops forming up can be accurately fixed about 20 yards south of where the present perpendicular crillon tower, built in 1530, now stands.

About 50 yards to the south-east of this tower, and standing alone in the large greensward, is a solitary granite block with a bronze plaque. It marks the area where Simon de Montfort was buried after the battle. The precise spot is not known but the visitor can be quite certain that he is within a very few yards of the grave.

The granite block was erected in 1965 when the seven-hundredth anniversary of the battle was commemorated. It was unveiled by the Speaker of the House of Commons and dedicated by the Archbishop of Canterbury, a fitting tribute by our democratic Parliament today to its founder of 700 years ago.

Bannockburn (1314)

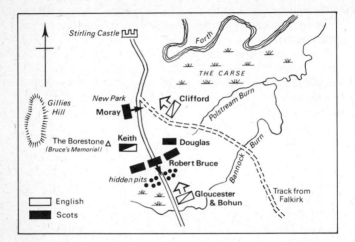

In 1272 Edward I succeeded to the throne of England. He had prudence, energy and, most importantly, foresight. He was one of the great English kings. In statesmanship he was far ahead of his time and he saw the danger of a hostile, virile, largely English-speaking nation on his northern border. He also saw the desirability of the four countries, England, Ireland, Scotland and Wales, making up the British Isles, being one country with one central government, although made up of four races.

As a start, Edward determined on the union of England and Scotland, and led several successful expeditions across the border against Scottish leaders of armies who were intent on defending their district and their country. He deposed Balliol by force and occupied many of the great barons' castles. Sir William Wallace, one of Scotland's great national heroes, led

expeditions to besiege them, but was captured and murdered.
Another patriot came on the stage, Robert the Bruce, 'King'
of Scotland.

Bruce had a considerable force of soldiers under his hand
and marched south. Edward marched to meet him, but died
suddenly. His successor, Edward II, was never the man to
face successfully the strong, warlike, dedicated Scottish
people, and step by step Bruce won his way. All the bigger
towns were reoccupied by his forces, and with one exception
the great castles were also reoccupied. Stirling Castle alone
held out, though closely invested by Bruce.

In 1314 Edward II led a huge army across the border.
Bruce with a far smaller army determined to give battle to the
'invader', to prevent Stirling being relieved. Bruce, outnumbered two to one, had two very strong cards in his pack
– the burning enthusiasm of patriots fighting on their native
soil to defend it, and the inadequacy of the military skill of
Edward II.

On 23 June Bruce had mustered some 7,000 men to resist
the English army advancing towards Stirling Castle. He had
several hours to select and prepare a good defensive position.
Both luck in finding one and skill in exploiting it were on his
side.

Three miles south of the castle a stream flows roughly
east–west, the Bannockburn. After a mile or so it veers away
to the north-east, and encloses a large marsh, the Carse by
name. It formed an excellent natural defensive obstacle and
Bruce rested his left flank on it. A mile north of the burn lay
a wood – New Park – another helpful feature for defence, and
Bruce took up his main position between it and the burn,
knowing that if retirement became necessary his infantry
could slip away to its shelter close behind them. Edward II's
cavalry would be at a great disadvantage, and very foolish, if
it tried to pursue infantry in a wood. The superiority of the

English army was not so considerable as its numbers implied.

Away to Bruce's right flank lay Gillies Hill, a sharp, easily seen feature, with sides of considerable declivity, dominating the battlefield. Prima facie it was a most desirable objective for the attackers, but it was covered with trees.

His two flanks resting on natural obstacles, his rear protected and a stream in front of him, Bruce had done well to find the site and to recognize its value. However, he was not satisfied and had dug large pits in the ground between the burn and the wood. In them pointed stakes were erected and above them the turf was relaid. Out beyond the pits ran the Bannockburn, 30 feet wide and its bank 10 feet deep: not a formidable obstacle in itself but sufficient to delay advancing infantry. The Scottish army took up position between the stream to their front and the wood to their rear.

At about 4 pm on the 23rd, Bruce and his men saw the English army approaching. One of the largest armies that a King of England had ever led and with a majority of mounted men, it must have made an awe-inspiring sight to the Scottish soldiers now resting behind their pits. The defenders on the walls of Stirling Castle, 2 miles away, must have seen their English comrades arriving to relieve them and have been greatly heartened by the magnificent sight.

By the time the English army had come up and concentrated for the attack it was too late to fight that day, and so both armies lay down in full view of each other to rest and await tomorrow's battle.

Next day, 24 June, the greatest day in Scottish history, the Scots 'stood to' at sunrise. About 8 am the English archers advanced across the Bannockburn. Bruce immediately sent his small but efficient cavalry force against them, and although the archers turned their fire on the horsemen the cavalry triumphed. The English bows were of no use at close quarters, and the Scottish horsemen, getting in among the enemy, were soon able to kill many and put the remainder to flight.

Edward II then ordered the whole of his force to charge against the Scottish front. The majority, being mounted, galloped forward on a wide front and rode into the unseen pits. The greatest chaos ensued. The front lines of horsemen went down into the pits and following lines were unseated, their horses trampling the survivors of the front lines. The Scots advanced and found the now dismounted cavalry an easy prey. The foot-soldiers armed with their pikes were able to kill every Englishman they found; the latter could not in many cases rise from the pits, or disentangle themselves from their plunging horses or rise quickly because of the weight of their armour.

The English infantry negotiated the pits and advanced towards the main Scottish position, but with little dash or impetus, and they were held by their enemy, determined not only to defeat the hated English but to drive them out of Scotland for ever.

The fighting now was round the pits. Both armies were locked in a death struggle.

Suddenly the English saw coming down the slopes of Gillies Hill a body of men carrying flying banners. It was only the servants, ghillies and camp-followers from Bruce's camp, who had occupied Gillies Hill as a grandstand to see the fight, but were no longer able to resist joining in. But the English troops, seeing this apparently new army advancing downhill on to their open left flank, lost heart and gave way. Sensibly Bruce kept his victorious army in hand and did not venture out of his position until quite certain that he would not be attacked again.

Many English soldiers, fleeing towards the town of Stirling to seek shelter, were drowned in the treacherous Carse. Others went towards the Firth of Forth, where, pursued by

The Bannockburn follows the line of straggling trees in middle distance. The pits were midway between the burn and the wire fence in the foreground.

Bruce's now released horsemen, they were driven into the river and there drowned. Many tried a direct flight to the rear, but in recrossing the Bannockburn were caught by other small parties of Scottish cavalry. Edward rode away and, by luck, found a boat at Dunbar to carry him safely to Berwick. This was the greatest victory the Scots ever gained.

Bannockburn is an outstanding example of a people fighting on their own soil to resist an invader – determined to win or die. Patriotism in the defence of the homeland is the most powerful of all weapons.

Today the battlefield of Bannockburn is easy to find. The National Trust for Scotland owns some 50 acres round the 'Borestone' on the top of the Bannock Brae where Bruce set up his standard. About 12 of these acres have been turned into a vast well-kept lawn. Just off the main road from Stirling to Falkirk is a new building where photographs of the area, wonderfully graphic plans of the battle and clear, brief accounts of the major points of the action are mounted on great notice-boards. In front of these boards is an excellent model of the battlefield as it was in 1314. There is also a well-equipped bookstall.

The visitor should walk up a well-kept path to the Rotunda – a large circular wall enclosing a monument built over the remains of the 'Borestone'. A few yards back from the Rotunda is a gigantic equestrian statue of Bruce, unveiled by the Queen in 1964.

New Park is now entirely denuded of trees and a housing estate completely covers the area of the wood that might have been so useful to Bruce had he been compelled to retire. These houses have come right up to the northern edge of the National Trust property, where they abruptly stop. Off to the north-west is Gillies Hill, still largely covered with trees.

Just to the front of Bruce's right flank was a considerable bog – 'Halberts Bog'. Its existence was probably not known to Edward II and had he advanced in that area he must have got into grave difficulties. Bruce doubtless found it and, avoiding it, used it as yet another natural obstacle in his favour.

The Burn meanders across the fields until it reaches the main Stirling–Falkirk road, where today it passes under a large bridge carrying the main road. In 1314 this road, one of the most important in Scotland, probably did not need a bridge to carry it over the shallow waterway and a ford was almost certainly all that was necessary.

The site of those historically notorious pits can be only very approximately conjectured. To the west of the road is open farmland and the pits could have been anywhere within 400 yards of the burn. To the east of the road, on a more probable site, a large housing estate has been built, and it is impossible to express any opinion as to where the pits might have been dug.

Close to the exhibition hall is the King Robert Hotel. Half-way down the main road to Bannockburn is the '1314 Inn', while farther up the road is the 'Borestone Bar'. The whole area is a Mecca for Scotsmen. The atmosphere of their great victory is everywhere. Some 80,000 visitors, mostly Scots, come yearly to see the battlefield.

Boroughbridge (1322)

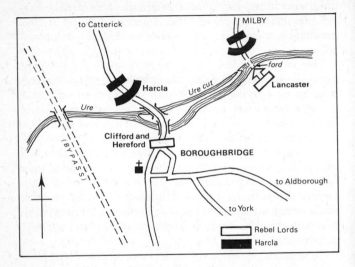

During the first 14 years of Edward II's reign England was
again split by the differences between the king and the barons.
Edward's father, Edward I, one of England's greatest kings,
easily kept the barons in check, but his son was not up to it.

By 1322 a strong group of barons had formed in opposition
to the king's feeble and corrupt government. They were led
by the Earl of Lancaster, Edward's uncle. Civil war broke
out, Lancaster raising an army of rebels in the north, moving
down to the Midlands. Edward marched up from the West
Country to meet them, pushing them back to the river Ure
at Boroughbridge.

Meanwhile Sir Andrew Harcla, Edward's warden of
Carlisle Castle, moved across the Pennines to meet them and,

hearing from a spy that Lancaster was making for Boroughbridge, he marched to contest the crossing, the only bridge
for 5 miles upstream or downstream, as it is today. On reaching Boroughbridge, Harcla held the bridge with his archers,
sending his spearmen to guard a ford half a mile downstream.
On arrival at Boroughbridge and on seeing his opponents,
Lancaster suggested to Harcla that he should come over with
his men and join the baronial rebels. The loyal Harcla
refused.

Lancaster then attacked the ford with his cavalry but was
unable to force it. Lords Clifford and Hereford had been sent
to carry the bridge and nearly succeeded, but one of Harcla's
men, possibly remembering a similar incident at Stamford
Bridge in 1066, secreted himself underneath the bridge and
killed Hereford as he crossed. Clifford was wounded and
Lancaster, returning from his failure at the ford, called off the
whole attack. Many of his men had deserted and he felt very
doubtful about his whole position. Not only was the local
military one precarious but his own political future, should
he be defeated, would surely end in death.

Surprisingly, Harcla allowed him to bivouac in the town,
on his side of the bridge, for the night. Next day Harcla
received reinforcements and crossing the then unguarded
bridge drove Lancaster and many of his subordinate knights
into the church. Some escaped dressed as peasants, but
Lancaster was captured and taken to Pontefract. Here he was
'tried' by Edward and immediately executed.

The ford is difficult to reach by car although a walk of about
800 yards along a path on the north bank of the river is of
interest because of the view of both sides of the river. It is
evident that below the ford it flowed through a marsh and
must have been virtually impassable, certainly by mounted

men. It is no wonder that Lancaster's cavalry could make no headway. As Harcla's men guarding the ford were spearmen with no archers, it is probable that no casualties on either side were suffered here.

From the map, and by examining the ground, it is evident that Lancaster was no soldier, certainly no tactician. To attack a river line, which is crossed by only two means, is not only suicidal but virtually impossible. Had he taken up a position across where Fisher Gate now stands he might have defeated Harcla by forcing him to tackle this disputed crossing within arrow range.

The 'new' bridge built in 1557, on the site of the old one

The inevitable failure would have given Lancaster the initiative and then allowed him to try the crossing himself. It is surprising that Harcla did not in his turn attempt to cross, having repulsed Lancaster. The answer probably lies in disparity of numbers. We know nothing whatever of the numbers engaged in this little battle, and the fact that one side, Lancaster's, was repulsed, that the victor did not pursue them and in fact allowed them to sleep unmolested in the town suggests that Harcla was in considerably inferior strength, and dare not risk another encounter with an enemy defeated but by no means routed.

The visitor to Boroughbridge can stand on the new bridge on the exact site of the 1322 bridge and there visualize the very simple action that took place within a few hundred square yards. A view upstream shows how difficult the crossing is today, while the photograph of the bridge itself shows the depth of the ravine.

No battle on British soil made less impact on British history than Boroughbridge. Its interest lies in the fact that it was fought precisely on one of the most famous roads in the British Isles, the A1. Hundreds of motorists cross the bridge daily and unknowingly pass through the centre of a battlefield.

Halidon Hill (1333)

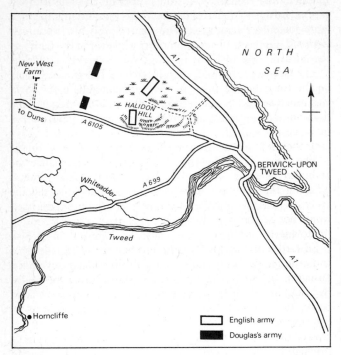

Robert Bruce, the victor of Bannockburn, died in 1329, being succeeded by his son, David II, then aged 7. The next four years saw a succession of five regents, acting in the minority of the king, each of whom warred, often successfully, against his predecessor. The third of these regents, Balliol, who had actually claimed and ascended the throne, was bundled off it by number four, Sir Andrew Moray, and evicted from Scotland across the Border.

Here Balliol remained at the centre of an intrigue and an English army, vowing to re-enter Scotland and reascend his throne. Edward III of England strongly supported him and a large force laid siege by both land and sea to the town of Berwick, the river Tweed, flowing through the town, being the border.

The Scottish army under Sir Archibald Douglas advanced on the town from the north but could not relieve it. There was much parleying, with little result, until the Scots in the town volunteered to surrender by a certain date unless relieved by some other Scots army beforehand. To show their good faith they sent out hostages to Balliol.

The Scots under Douglas, now disgruntled at their inability to relieve the town, moved off to the west, burning and pillaging the countryside and hoping to draw the English army after them. But Edward III, now in supreme command, would not be drawn, and the English army remained investing the town.

Edward lost patience with the stubbornness of the defence and cruelly, and with entire loss of faith, hanged one of the hostages, the son of Sir Alexander Seton, the governor of Berwick, in full view of the town. Douglas, hearing of this barbarity, returned from his foray into Northumberland, determined to fight a pitched battle with the English. He crossed the Tweed at Coldstream and, moving on to the north, reached Duns, 12 miles to the west of Berwick. Edward accepted the challenge and crossing the Tweed near Horncliffe took up a position on Halidon Hill, 2 miles out of Berwick, astride the Duns–Berwick road (the A6105 today) facing north-west. On the left was Balliol's division: King Edward commanded the centre, while Sir Edward Bohun's group was on the right.

At the foot of the hill, 600 feet high, a marsh ran along its northern face. The ground was, and still is, completely open and from the top of the hill Edward could see Berwick below and behind him and could observe every direction from which Douglas might advance. Edward's line ran roughly along the present wire fence, midway between the top of the hill and the near edge of the bog.

Douglas coming down the Duns road could see the English on Halidon Hill, in front of him. After crossing Mordington Bridge, $1\frac{1}{2}$ miles from Edward's position, he turned left off the main road close to New West Farm and moved across the open country. About halfway between the farm and the hilltop he blundered into the marsh.

At once his cavalry advance guard became bogged down and the men had to dismount. Their horses were taken to the rear behind the shelter of Witches Knowe, a mile away – a foolish move, as at that distance from the battlefield they could exert no influence on the engagement. During the confusion caused by the removal of the horses, the infantry passed through the now dismounted horsemen. The English archers opened concentrated and rapid fire at this excellent target. The Scotsmen floundered on and, emerging breathless from the marsh, tried to climb the hill.

In their attack up the hill very few Scots could really get near the defending English firing line and their main weapon, the pike, was of little value against the skilled archers whom they could not reach. Those gallant few who did reach the English line were hopelessly outnumbered and quickly killed.

The English knights who had prudently kept their horses just behind the brow of the hill now remounted and, galloping down the hill and round the marsh, chased the Scotsmen back to Duns. Seventy noblemen, including Douglas himself, 500 dismounted knights and several thousand foot-soldiers, were killed, while Edward lost only one knight and six infantrymen. Had the horses of the Scots been close at hand their riders, now remounted, might have held off the pursuing English cavalry, allowing many of the foot-soldiers to escape. But their absence meant that there was little resistance. The English were no braver than their enemy and in fact were fewer in number. But their disciplined fire and a good tactical position gave them an immense and winning advantage.

This battlefield is easily found and inspected. Take the A6105 from Berwick-on-Tweed, and leave the car at the brow of the hill, two miles before reaching Duns. A steep walk through the farmyard leads into the big grass field where the next farmhouse to the left can be seen. The visitor is now in the middle of the English position; behind him is Halidon Hill itself, and the only ploughed field anywhere near and immediately in front is the bog. All the remaining fields round are under grass and the bog is very obvious. It was drained some years ago and is now rich arable land, but the farmer. says that if the field drains get blocked the original marsh quickly shows itself.

It is easy to visualize the chaos caused by Douglas's cavalry floundering into the morass, the horses being led away, the infantry struggling through the sodden ground, their breathless climb up the considerable slope, all in the face of English archers, who only 13 years later were to win Crécy by their superb fire discipline.

A short drive for another half a mile along the A6105 and then a right turn up the hill to New West Farm brings the visitor to a second viewpoint. A walk through the farmyard southwards and then a climb up the rising ground, plough or pasture, gives an excellent stand to see the battlefield as Douglas saw it. The bog is even more apparent, its present dark ploughed soil showing clearly amid the light green grass all round.

The bog, and the fine discipline of the English archers in their magnificent tactical position, gave the more numerous Scots no chance. On no battlefield described in this book is the inevitable result more apparent.

Neville's Cross (1346)

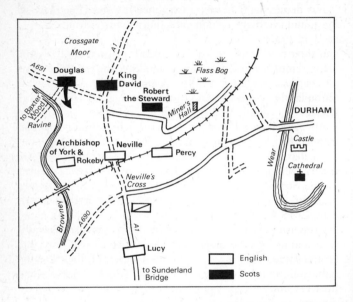

In mid-July 1346 Edward III disembarked near Cherbourg with his English army. Ostensibly his invasion was to secure the throne of France, but in reality he looked for a great adventure and to enjoy revenge against the French king who had repudiated his claim to the throne.

Two months later the French king, after his devastating defeat by the English at Crécy in August, and in near despair, called on his ally, David II of Scotland, to invade England and thus, he hoped, force Edward to send some troops home to meet the Scottish invasion. David agreed, believing that intervention over the border must bring respite to the French and, anyway, an attack on England was always popular, and an excuse for one could easily be found.

His descendant, James IV, took exactly the same view in 1513, and invaded England while Henry VIII was leading an army in France. Both David II and James IV were defeated and their respective attempts to take advantage of England's being temporarily denuded of troops were dismal failures.

King David crossed the border and after harrying Northumberland reached Durham in mid-October, his army 18,000 strong.

An English army in the north of 15,000 men was commanded by the Archbishop of York, Lord Neville and Henry, Lord Percy. It assembled at Bishop Auckland, very near the enemy, who were at Durham, only 11 miles away.

The Scots had an outpost at Sunderland Bridge, 3 miles south of Durham, on the modern A1 where it crosses the main LMS London–Edinburgh railway line. Neville, leading the English advance guard northwards, brushed the outpost aside and led the English army along the present A1. He took up a position facing north more or less along the present main railway line from, on the left, the rail bridge over the river Browney, to about Miners' Hall on Flass Street. On the left of the line was the archbishop, with Neville in the centre along Redhills Lane, Percy being near the Miners' Hall. Each division had a party of archers out in front.

About 700 yards away the Scots formed up, King David in the centre, also astride the A1 and opposite Neville. On the Scots' right was the division of the Earl of Douglas, whose position, prima facie, seems good, his outer flank resting on the deep ravine through which the river Browney flows. But this ravine has several considerable curves and one such curve obtruded sharply across Douglas's front.

The Scots attacked first and at once got into difficulties because the ravine suddenly narrows the front. Douglas's men were pushed into the flank and centre of King David's division. The terrain was uneven anyway and near chaos ensued in this area. At once the English archers opened fire, causing many casualties, as well as halting the advance.

On the Scots' left the division led by Robert, the Steward of Scotland, had some success, and pushed back slightly Neville's and Percy's men. The battle-line halted and then Neville ordered forward the cavalry round his right flank. Not expecting this manoeuvre, the Scots' left recoiled sharply. The archbishop advanced against the still confused Scottish right flank and pushing them back caused many to be drowned in the river Browney. King David's division in the centre was almost surrounded, and collapsed, the king being captured while trying to escape over the Browney Bridge at Baxter Woods, by the present sewage works. The Scots were defeated again.

Today the ravine that caused so much dislocation in the Red Hill area is much built round. A good impression of its depth is obtained from the bridge leading to Baxter Wood. To find it, pass over the great Neville's Cross crossroads on the A1 and bear left after half a mile down Toll House Road. Four hundred yards farther the turning into the ravine is signposted as 'Baxter Wood'.

A brief halt on the A1 at Quarry House Lane, where the road crosses the railway line, is not without interest. Despite the mass of buildings, the visitor can be quite certain that he is standing exactly where Neville's left flank stood before its slight withdrawal.

Percy's position ran from the north side of Miners' Hall along the line of Redhills Terrace overlooking the present magnificent playing-fields of Johnston Grammar School. Beyond them to the north is the broken ground which added to King David's and Douglas's dislocation, previously caused by the ravine's unexpected curve.

The magnificent Norman towers of the cathedral, less than a mile away from the battlefield, were of course standing in 1346, and doubtless were occupied by the bishop and mayor, watching the battle. They must have been very apprehensive as to the fate of the cathedral and its riches, and the old town generally, in the event of a Scottish victory.

Rottingdean (1377)

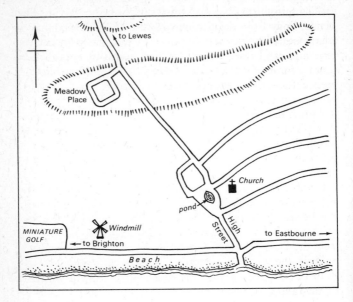

Few people have heard of the Battle of Rottingdean of 1377. It was a raid by French pirates which lasted only 36 hours, and penetrated barely 3 miles inland. Yet scars of the fracas are still visible in the church today.

During the latter half of the fourteenth century similar raids were made on Newhaven, Southampton, Portsmouth, Plymouth and Hastings. Surprisingly Dover was not attacked, although it was the easiest port to reach from the French coast.

It seems probable that the cause of these raids was a subconscious hatred of the English because of their victories at

Crécy and Poitiers only 31 and 21 years previously. There was no central government in France at that time, and the various self-governing states of Brittany, Anjou, Normandy, Maine, Poitou and so on were far too disorganized to mount a large-scale retaliatory invasion. It was therefore left for the pirates to carry out their own little forays and revenge their country for Poitiers. The capture of their king, John, who had been released from England after Poitiers only 18 years before, was an insult which still rankled.

During the summer of 1377 several hundred pirates landed at the Gap at Rottingdean which, with its flanking chalk cliffs, was in the fourteenth century at least 800 yards farther out to sea than it is now, and well beyond the present low-water mark.

Possibly the goal of the raid was Lewes Priory and the riches which the great religious houses of those days owned. But Lewes is 6 miles from Rottingdean across the Downs, and at least 8 miles following the easier way up the valley running from the Gap. Unless the French had a large force, which is unlikely, the project of reaching Lewes would be so hazardous as to be improbable and a hit-and-run raid doing as much damage and creating as much annoyance as possible in a short time seems a more common-sense plan.

Having landed unexpectedly, the pirates quickly caused chaos in the village and in the narrow main street it is easy to visualize the burning, looting, destruction and murder that were committed. Many of the villagers fled to the village church standing on high ground where the houses finished and the Downs began. Its Saxon tower, standing today as in 1377, was clearly visible from many parts of the village. By far the most substantial building, it would naturally draw the terrified people to its shelter.

A horseman galloped off over the Downs to Lewes Priory to warn the prior. A valiant and dominating man, he at once

took control and gathered together a large number of countrymen, doubtless armed only with scythes, pitchforks, bill-
hooks and axes, and marched them down the valley to engage
the pirates. All this must have taken some time, and points to
the probability of the raid lasting at least 36 hours.

Meanwhile, the few survivors in the church had climbed
into the belfry and pulled up the ladder. Here they were seen
by the pirates, who set fire to the church. All those in the
belfry perished. The scorch-marks left by the flames can be
clearly seen on three of the four pillars supporting the tower
and its belfry. Together with those murdered in the village,
about 100 people died in Rottingdean that day. Its total
population would not have been more than about 300.

Early next morning the pirates moved out of the village
northwards to meet the prior's force coming down from
Lewes. A considerable clash between the two unorganized
forces occurred, possibly on both sides of the road, and along
the piece of high ground where Meadow Place runs off to the
left. There is no actual evidence, however, as to where the
battle took place and it could have been on the next ridge
farther north towards Lewes.

In the battle the prior was captured, together with two subordinate knights, Sir John Fallisle and Sir Thomas Chinie,
but the French also suffered heavily and withdrew to the Gap
for re-embarkation. They took a lot of plunder from the
village and the three important prisoners of war, but these
latter were later released after large ransoms had been paid.
It seems unlikely that the large ransom could have been
collected in time from the few villagers left alive before the
pirates sailed away and, therefore, the three unfortunate
prisoners must have been carried back to France. It is improbable that a deputation would later cross over to Normandy with the cash, hoping to find the three men, so the
release must have been engineered by the government. The

The church, with its tower and belfry, burnt by the pirates

three men cannot have felt very happy or optimistic while in the hands of the pirates, nor could their expectation of life have been very great.

A visit to Rottingdean should include a visit to the Gap, although it is now so far back from the original pirates' landing-place. The church, with its scarred pillars and its belfry, and the narrow main street where so much horror was experienced, are full of interest. Few people in Rottingdean seem to know of this admittedly unimportant little facet of English history. One middle-aged shopkeeper, born, bred and educated in the village, admitted that she had never heard of it, yet the author's wife, whose family lived at Telscombe, remembers being warned as a child about the bogey of the pirates of Rottingdean, if she were naughty.

Otterburn (1388)

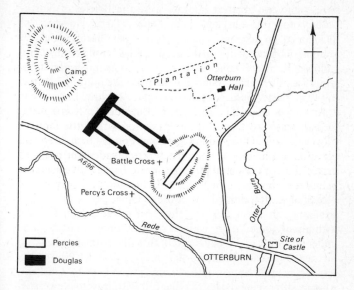

One of the effects of Hadrian's Wall had been to create a no-man's-land to the north of it, of bare, open rolling moors, sparsely populated. The area was of little agricultural value and apart from the grazing of cattle and sheep was unproductive. But the area terminating at the wall had become the traditional frontier between England and Scotland and saw countless raids by the countrymen of both sides. The inhabitants were almost continuously at war and had been for centuries, even though their respective governments might be at peace.

The raids into each other's territory were made by the lesser chiefs, largely for food and cattle and sheep rustling.

The great nobles, being very wealthy, did not have to make such raids for their subsistence but they, too, had their family feuds. The two greatest families were the Percies of Northumberland, the son and heir being Harry Hotspur – so nicknamed on account of his fiery temper, hard riding and dominating personality – and the Douglas family from round Liddesdale, near Dalkeith. It was said that no leader from either family, hearing that someone from the other family was in the vicinity, could refrain from attacking him.

In 1388 Richard II was King of England. He was a weak, foolish, dissolute man, a poor successor to his great father, Edward III, in whose reign Crécy and Poitiers had been won. Nevertheless he took it upon himself to invade Scotland with little or no *casus belli* and burnt several abbeys in the Lowlands before withdrawing.

Scotland, determined on revenge, sent two armies on a retaliatory invasion. One to the west advanced on Carlisle with about 30,000 men, while a smaller force of about 5,000 under the Earl of Douglas acted as a diversionary attack on the east and, crossing the border, made a dash for Newcastle. Passing round the town this army pushed on to Durham, whence, after several days of pillage, it withdrew to Newcastle. Here lay the Earl of Northumberland's army, the Percies unwilling to make a sortie against Douglas in case he was only the vanguard of the great Scottish army they knew had been raised.

Douglas had no siege machinery of any sort with which to reduce the great walls of Newcastle, one of the strongest towns in the north of England. But it was unthinkable for a Percy and a Douglas to wait with armed men under their command, glowering at each other across a wall, and not attack. Percy sent out a challenge to Douglas to meet him in personal combat. An arena was laid out and the two great nobles met in a mounted duel. Percy was unhorsed but Douglas refrained from killing him as he lay on the ground, as the laws of chivalry allowed, and contented himself with tearing the pennon from Percy's spear and fixing it to his own. Challenging Percy to come and fetch it, he led his army back to the border.

Percy then heard that the main Scottish force was nowhere near, and in fact was at Carlisle. Realizing that he thus had parity in numbers with Douglas, he left Newcastle hotly pursuing the retreating Scots.

Douglas halted at Otterburn, 32 miles north of Newcastle. Here, about a mile north of the village, he pitched his tent, in front of which he stuck his spear in the ground with Percy's pennon flying; he then moved forward to a position on a little hill half a mile in front. Some primitive fortifications were dug.

About midday next day, 19 August, Percy's army approached, halting just to the north of West Townhead Farm to allow him to divide his force in two. Leading in person he then attacked across the fields in mass with infantry and archers, while sending Sir Thomas Umfraville with 3,000 mounted men round in a great detour to come down on the left and rear of Douglas's army.

Percy's frontal attack was successful at first and his superior numbers gradually drove the Scots back up the hill towards their camp behind them. It became a detailed hand-to-hand fight with swords, axes and pikes, and the men became so mixed up that the English archers were unable to shoot for fear of killing their own men.

Douglas, seeing that his smaller numbers were getting the worst of it, now decided to do what Richard III was to try at Bosworth 100 years later. He rode into the enemy himself with a small escort. Richard was to fail and meet his death, but Douglas succeeded. Inspiring his men by his own example to stand and fight, he turned the tide and led them forward. Tragically, he was mortally wounded but, knowing the usual adverse effect on morale when a leader is killed, ordered his body to be carried into the shelter of a patch of bracken, unseen.

By now it was growing dark and the Scots, not knowing of Douglas's death, fought on all through the night. The English, feeling the shock of the Scottish advance, sparked off by Douglas's brave gesture, withdrew a little and the advancing Scots put the English to ruin. Both Percies, the Earl and Hotspur, were captured and both sides lay down exhausted to sleep towards dawn. Umfraville, who had found Douglas's camp empty, achieved nothing and slowly returned the way he had come, reaching at dawn the English army sleeping in the village of Otterburn; he led them back to Newcastle. Had he shown more aggression on finding Douglas's camp deserted and returned to the area to fight, he might have caught the flank and rear of the Scotsmen and turned Percy's undoubted defeat into a victory.

Eighteen thousand Englishmen were killed but more important was the vast number of prisoners taken. Among them were many wealthy and famous knights from Northumbria. Their ransoms raised a number of impoverished Scottish families to affluence for many years.

The Battle of Otterburn was really only a contest between two great, and antagonistic, families. It had no effect whatever on history and had the battle gone the other way and Percy been the winner, life on the border would have been quite unchanged. It gained notoriety largely thanks to 'The Ballad of Chevy Chase', written by an unknown author some years after the battle. The author depicts an English victory.

The choice of the words 'Chevy Chase' is inexplicable. There is no wood, moor, hill or stream of that name in the district and the local people do not know why the battle was called thus. Curiously enough there is a wood named 'Chevy Chase' less than a mile from the battlefield of Shrewsbury, fought 15 years later in 1403, where the English were the victors and in which Hotspur, Percy's son, was killed. The defeated Scots were in fact chased through this wood by Henry IV's cavalry and the suspicion is inescapable that the author of the ballad confused the two battles. Perhaps Otterburn has been living in a false notoriety for 600 years, while Shrewsbury has modestly accepted the lesser limelight.

To find the battlefield, bear right at a big garage at the western exit of the village on the A696, up a second-class road. Four hundred yards up this road is a big farmstead on

West Townhead Farm is in the middle distance. The English took up a line approximately along the line of the wall. Immediately in front is one of the four, possibly burial, mounds, which are out of character with the surrounding fields

the left, West Townhead; walk through the farmyard and out over the fields along a clearly defined grass-covered cart-track. After 400 yards the cart-track peters out where four substantial stone walls meet, and this is the centre of the battlefield. Immediately to the north of this wall-junction are four or five large grass-covered mounds, about 4 feet high, and quite out of character with all the surrounding land, which is flat. These mounds are equal in area to a tennis court, and cannot be the last vestiges of the primitive defensive works dug by Douglas. They form no sort of a line or tactical plan. As they are in the very centre of the battlefield it is not impossible that they are burial mounds and excavation may uncover bones and perhaps metal. Wood, leather and cloth will have long since rotted away.

Eight hundred yards north-west is the hill, marked on the 2½-inch map as 'tumulus', where Douglas pitched his camp.

The views all round are superb and for them alone the walk along the muddy cart-track is well worth while.

Shrewsbury (1403)

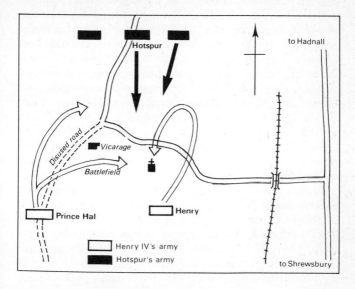

The cause of the Wars of the Roses lay in one question. When Richard II was deposed in 1399, had Henry Bolingbroke, the son of Edward III's third son, a better claim to the throne than his uncle Edmund, Duke of York, Edward's fourth son? Was it uncle or nephew? (Both ignored the true heir, Edward's great grandson by his second son, Lionel of Clarence.)

Bolingbroke ruthlessly seized the throne and at once threw the rival claimant, the able, lusty, popular Edmund of York, and his followers into active opposition. Henry and Edmund started the Wars of the Roses – to last until the final overthrow of the House of York at Bosworth 85 years later.

Henry Bolingbroke was crowned Henry IV in 1399. He

reigned for only 14 years, dying at the age of 46. His undoubted usurpation of the throne made him several powerful
enemies, who resented his exclusion of the rightful claimant.
One of these enemies was Henry Percy, Earl of Northumberland, head of the most powerful family in the north of
England.

The Percies had a long-standing feud with the Glendowers
of Wales. Percy asked Henry for money to carry on the feud
and as a bribe suggested that it would keep Glendower quiet.
Glendower was becoming very powerful in Wales and it was
not impossible that he might lead a national rising. Henry
refused, however, and Percy at once completely changed his
attitude – he marched south to join forces with Glendower
and, united, to fight the king.

Henry marched to Shrewsbury where his young son,
Shakespeare's famous Prince Hal, later the romantic Henry V
of Agincourt, had a small army. Hearing that 'Hotspur',
Percy's son, had, with an army of 10,000, left Chester to the
south, Henry and young Hal took up a position facing north
along some high ground now known as Battlefield, 3 miles
north of Shrewsbury, to bar Hotspur's road. Their line ran
from the present A49, Shrewsbury–Hadnall, near the junction
of that road with the third-class road running due west to the
church, and passed 200 yards south of the church, which did
not exist in 1403. Three-quarters of a mile to the north of the
church is a large wood called Chevy Chase, but there seems
to be no connection between this unusual name and the battle
fought in Northumberland 15 years previously and 170 miles
away. None of the locals seem to know anything about this
curious fact.

As Henry's men were forming up Hotspur's army was
occupying considerably higher ground opposite, about 500
yards away along the southern edge of Ash Walk Coppice. It
covered a frontage of 800 yards and lay along the ridge 400

yards north of the present church. When all was ready the
Abbot of Shrewsbury passed from one army to the other
hoping to arrange some settlement of the argument, but to
no avail. The royal army advanced, and now occurred a
genuine fire-fight. The king's longbowmen halted and opened
fire when they reached a line just to the north of the present
church. Hotspur's men returned the fire skilfully and
effectively and greatly dismayed the royal regulars, who were
expecting a walkover against an army which they knew had
only recently been recruited and had little training. Their aim
became ragged and their rate of fire slowed. After a heavy
exchange of fire the royal army withdrew in some disorder.

Mr and Mrs Evans' house and the pond, between which Young Hal
charged, from the left

Hotspur seized his advantage and advanced down the slope, his men at arms catching many of the archers. At the bottom of the rise Henry's men stopped and faced about, whereupon a general mêlée ensued round the ponds in front of and on either side of the present church and the house owned by Mr and Mrs Evans. Hotspur, with 30 knights, tried to hack his way through the fight to reach and dispatch the king, as had happened at Hastings, but Henry's chief of staff saw the possibility and persuaded him to leave the danger zone. Meanwhile, Prince Hal's division out on the left had suffered little from the arrow fight and now saw its chance to take some part. It advanced and attacked Hotspur's right flank

'Battlefield' church, built by Henry IV in 1408

between the westernmost pond and Mr Evans's house. Pushing on, it got behind the enemy, who were thus threatened from the rear, from their right, and of course from the undefeated king's army, with which they were closely embroiled, to their front. In the course of this now indescribable chaos Hotspur was felled by an arrow and, as usual in medieval battles, the elimination of a leader resulted in wholesale collapse and retreat. Henry advanced again and, sending his cavalry in, pursued Hotspur's men for 3 miles, to total victory.

Today the site of the battle is easy to find, to visit and to see, the best viewpoint being the lane from the church to Mr Evans's house (marked on the 2½-inch ordnance map as 'vicarage'). The pond is still there, about 30 yards by 20, and is never dry even after the longest drought. On its bank are two hoary gnarled old oaks, possibly young trees in 1403.

The church was built by Henry IV in 1408 in memory of the fallen on both sides. Much of the original stained glass remains, and high up in the clerestory are very old replicas of the shields of Henry, his son young Hal, and about 20 of his knights. Outside, on the eastern gable, high up, is a carved stone statue of Henry. It has never been removed and is, of course, much weather-beaten.

Apart from the church, Mr Evans's house and the next farm higher up the ridge, all is as it was in 1403. Hedges have appeared, of course. (Hedges are quite a modern invention, not having been used or planted until the eighteenth century.) No speculation is needed whatsoever at the battlefield of Shrewsbury. Everything is in view of the visitor.

First St Albans (1455)

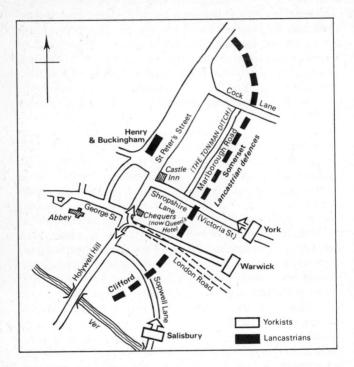

The Wars of the Roses were really a private quarrel between the reigning Lancastrians under Henry VI – and Richard, Duke of York, Henry's third cousin. The first opening for the Yorkists came when Henry, emerging from one of his fits of insanity, banished Richard to Yorkshire and appointed the Duke of Somerset as his chief adviser. Richard at once took action, chiefly against Somerset, and with his great friend, the

Earl of Warwick, 'the Kingmaker', marched south with 3,000 men.

In reply Henry and Somerset marched from London with 2,000 men via Watford and St Stephens, reaching St Albans at 7 am on 20 May.

Immediately they started to erect a stockade along the Tonman Ditch, standing to the east of the town. York's army arrived from Royston via Ware and Hatfield, settling down for some sleep outside the ditch in Key Fields, opposite the Lancastrians. At 9 am York sent messengers to King Henry, stating that if the king would surrender Somerset, whom York considered a traitor, he, York, would not attack and in fact would withdraw. When the king refused, York attacked.

Across Victoria Street and Sopwell Lane the barricades erected along the Tonman Ditch held for a while. The Yorkists then launched three separate operations. On the right an out-flanking move across Hatfield Road penetrated the ditch, and reached St Peter's Street near Burroughgate, there turning left. On the left a breach was made near Sopwell Lane, while the main centre attack advanced up both sides of Victoria Street and the present London Road, reaching the market place which the present town hall overlooks. Here King Henry had his headquarters, and here the most serious and bloody fighting took place, the Lancastrians being pressed from the north, from the south and at the centre from Victoria Street. Somerset was killed on the steps of the Castle Inn at the corner of Victoria Street and the market place, and the king, already wounded, was captured. The Lancastrian army disintegrated and Henry was led away through the abbey gateway (still standing today) to the abbot's house, where his wound was dressed. Next day he left for London.

Today, along the west side of Upper Marlborough Road, a large bank of earth can be seen. This is the soil from the

Tonman Ditch along which the present road was built.
Opposite No. 22 a gap in the retaining wall of the bank shows
the materials used in building the original bank. This bank
can just be traced again where it passes over the present
Sopwell Lane, farther south.

Key Fields, where the Yorkists spent a few hours asleep
before the battle, are now covered by houses and gardens on
both sides of Lattimer Road.

The line of the present buildings along the eastern side of
Holywell Hill, Chequer Street, the market place, and St
Peter's Street are exactly on the sites of similar medieval
buildings of 1455. Indeed all round the market place the
layout of the streets today is identical with that existing at the
time of the battle. The site of the Castle Inn is now occupied
by the National Westminster Bank, on a wall of which is a
plaque recording the death of Somerset.

In St Peter's churchyard are buried many soldiers of both
sides, the graves being just to the north of the church.

Northampton (1460)

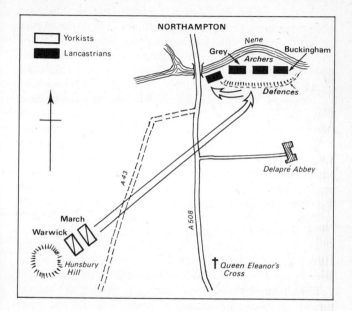

In 1460 the Lancastrian army with King Henry VI and
Queen Margaret had moved to Northampton, to occupy a
position in a bend of the river Nene immediately south of the
town. The Yorkists, under Warwick the Kingmaker, marched
up to the Midlands to find them.

Prima facie the Lancastrian position was good but the river
behind is deep and in October 1460 was swollen after rain.
Lord Grey held the right flank, near where the present road
from Buckingham, the A508, crosses the river at the beginning
of Bridge Street. In the centre were the archers. On the left
stood the Duke of Buckingham's group. The entrenchments

were strengthened with pointed stakes, an idea copied from Agincourt.

Warwick and Prince Edward, up from London with some 4,000 men, spent the night on Hunsbury Hill. At dawn they advanced against the Lancastrian position, crossing the present A43 from Towcester diagonally and then the present A508 from London very near Queen Eleanor's Cross. By Queen Eleanor's Cross stood the Archbishop of Canterbury and the papal legate from Rome, who saw the White Rose army pass before them. They had arrived from London to arbitrate between Warwick and Margaret, without success.

The ground was heavy in the rain and the pace of Prince Edward's mounted infantry was very slow. As they came within range they met heavy arrow fire from the Lancastrian centre group. The defending guns were so soaked in the rain that their charges could not be ignited, but archery and the pointed stakes looked like holding up those of Edward's cavalry who were surviving the arrow fire. A stalemate seemed likely. Suddenly treachery appeared in the Royalist ranks. Lord Grey ordered his men to surrender, and indeed to show Prince Edward's men a weak spot in the stockade. The Yorkists poured through the gap and, passing behind the archers, attacked Buckingham's inner flank. All the Lancastrians turned and fled. Across the swollen river was the only way out, but many were drowned. Buckingham was killed, the king was captured and Margaret and their son, Prince Edward, escaped to Scotland. Richard of York, who was not present at the battle, claimed the throne when Warwick returned to London.

Nearly all the area on which fighting took place is now covered with railway sidings. However, the approximate line of the stakes can be surmised from a good standpoint, a loading ramp 5 feet high in the railway yard. From the bridge the river is seen to be entirely bounded by large factories. Even with the canalization that has taken place, the river is still 30 yards wide, and in 1460 was probably double that width, though shallower. The line of advance from Hunsbury Hill diagonally across the two roads is entirely covered by a vast housing estate and it is impossible to say exactly where the Yorkists crossed the two roads.

Queen Eleanor's Cross on its considerable and artificial mound is easily found about 2 miles south of the bridge on the A508, the sculpture being in a remarkably good condition. It was standing in 1460 and its mound provided a good viewpoint from which the archbishop and the legate could see the Yorkist army passing some 500 yards away.

Wakefield (1460)

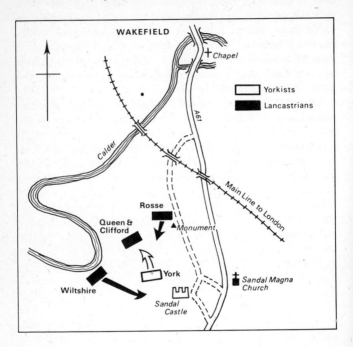

Queen Margaret heard after the Yorkist victory at Northampton that Richard of York and his son had been proclaimed the next heirs to the throne, instead of her own son.

Infuriated at this unlawful exclusion she marched south with 18,000 men to near Wakefield, with many Yorkist deserters. These had joined her when York was proclaimed heir, not because they preferred the young untried prince, but because he was the lawful heir. The English have always liked legitimacy.

Hearing of Margaret's aggression Richard of York came up from London with 5,000 men, while Prince Edward went into Wales to recruit.

Margaret took up a position 2 miles south of Wakefield. Here she posted a strong detachment on Sandal Common in view of Sandal Castle, where she knew York and his army were billeted. The remainder of her force she held back under Lord Clifford. On the right was the Earl of Wiltshire; Clifford commanded the centre with Queen Margaret 'listening in', while Lord Rosse commanded the cavalry out of sight on the left.

Richard of York was anxious to repeat the success of Northampton and decided to attack at once, although two of his older and more experienced subordinates strongly advised caution.

However York would not wait and he launched a head-on attack with all his forces at Clifford's centre. Its impact broke the Lancastrian line and the centre group under Clifford became deeply involved in the ensuing mêlée. Clifford was a skilled tactician and saw that although York's attacking force was in the ascendency temporarily, he had no reserve. Accordingly he ordered Wiltshire's force on the right to advance and then swing inwards on to Richard's left flank. He then released Rosse's cavalry, which advanced, enveloping the White Rose right. The Yorkist army, after its promising start was now surrounded and cut to pieces Sandal Castle was captured and many Yorkists, trying to find shelter in Wakefield, were killed by Rosse's pursuing cavalry. One, Richard of York's eldest son, was caught by Clifford himself on Wakefield bridge and there murdered, the boy having surrendered. Clifford claimed that he was justified, as his father had been killed by York at St Albans 5 years previously.

The Duke of York himself was killed, with 2,900 of his men, among them the old Earl of Salisbury. Prima facie the

Yorkist cause seemed to have lost its leaders at Wakefield, but two great Yorkists lived, Edward IV to be and his brother, later Richard III.

The battle was fought just to the west of Sandal Castle, which can be easily reached via Pinfold Grove on the A61 and then to the foot of Castle Hill. An easy but muddy walk brings one to the very considerable hill on which the castle ruins stand and are being excavated. A superb view is obtained and no other point need be visited on the actual battlesite. Everything can be seen from the castle.

The chapel on Wakefield Bridge, still standing, was endowed by Edward IV in memory of his brother, murdered on the bridge. The foundations and first 6 feet of masonry are prior to 1462 but the main walls and roof were rebuilt in the Gothic style in 1874.

A service is held in the chapel every Sunday afternoon. It is a cherished possession of Wakefield. The bridge, entirely rebuilt, occupies the exact site of the original wooden construction of 1460.

Mortimer's Cross (1461)

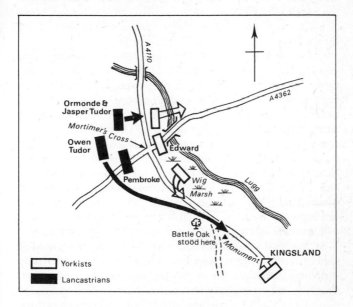

Prince Edward of York, Earl of March and later to be Edward IV, was not present at the Battle of Wakefield on New Year's Eve 1460. His father, the 3rd Duke of York, leader of the Yorkists, and his elder brother, Prince Edmund, the Earl of Rutland, had marched north to meet Queen Margaret and had sent young Prince Edward to Wales, there to recruit men for the Yorkist cause into a new Welsh army.

Early in January news of the death of his father and the murder of his brother at the Battle of Wakefield reached Edward in Wales and was a terrible shock to the 19-year-old boy. The defeat of the Yorkists at Wakefield had naturally shaken him, and he knew that all Lancastrian leaders and their followers in the west of England would be after him. Warwick the Kingmaker was far away in London, picking up the pieces of the Yorkist party and army after its Wakefield disaster, and Edward was indeed alone and far from home.

However in Wales he had some success. His recruits were yeoman farmers from the Welsh borders, well mounted and good horsemen. Among them there were a few townsmen from Ludlow, Leominster and Presteign. All were poorly armed and had little training, but possessed great morale. They thought highly of Edward. His strength of character, some charm of manner, reasonably good looks and, of course, a definite claim to the throne, all combined to make him a leader that men would follow. He ruled England for 12 years, and led the Yorkists to victory at Mortimer's Cross, Towton Moor, Barnet and Tewkesbury. He was England's greatest 'soldier-king' and it is sad that his moral character in middle and later life fell far short of his other great qualities.

At the end of January Edward had collected his very sketchy army round Hereford. To escape the numerically superior Lancastrian forces moving towards Worcester from the west and trying to come between him and London, he moved away to the north for 17 miles and reached a crossroads deep in the Herefordshire countryside. Here the river Lugg, flowing south to join the Wye, having passed through a steep-sided defile, emerges into flatter ground. Here at the cross-roads are a few cottages, a hotel and a bridge over the river. Edward placed his army between the road up from Hereford, the river, the bridge and the crossroads and waited.

On 2 February at daybreak a Lancastrian force came up the road from the west through Shobdon under the command of the Earl of Pembroke. A strong attack under the Earl of Ormonde against Edward's right group round the weir 300 yards north of the crossroads succeeded in pushing it back to the river, where it disintegrated. The middle Lancastrian brigade, under Pembroke himself, at the same time attacked the Yorkist centre under Edward's personal command at, and to the south of, the crossroads, but was repulsed, with very heavy loss. Ormonde's successful left-wing group returned to the field to reinforce Pembroke, but on arrival found him defeated. They then sat down and waited on events.

The last uncommitted Lancastrian group on the right flank, under Owen Tudor, now tried to move round the Yorkists' left flank, near where New House Farm now stands. But Edward's left group, so far without a fight, advanced on the exposed left flank of this attempted outflanking Lancastrian manoeuvre and cut it in two. The whole attacking army now collapsed, most of the defeated Lancastrians retreating south-east down the present A4110 to Leominster; Edward, moving forward, had difficulty in restraining his men from killing the wounded. Owen Tudor was captured and executed in Hereford market place. He was the grandfather of Henry VII, our first Tudor monarch.

This quite unimportant little battle of the Wars of the Roses has only two noteworthy facts. It gave Edward experience in commanding in battle an independent force and thus paved the way for his three other great successes. Secondly it is a battlefield that is easily found and comfortably examined; it can be seen in its entirety from the excellent viewpoint of the bridge 200 yards to the east of the crossroads.

Immediately over the bridge, on slightly rising ground and only 150 yards from the field where most of the fighting took place, stands today an occupied cottage. Its lowermost southerly two rooms, the original building, were built in 1450. Its occupant must have seen the action from a ring-side seat.

Second St Albans (1461)

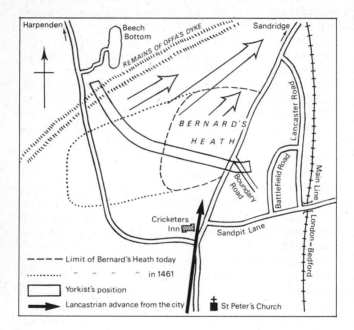

After Queen Margaret's victory at Wakefield she moved south with a large army, ravaging the country on a 30-mile front. Grantham, Stamford, Peterborough, Huntingdon and Royston all felt her heavy hand. Her tardy advance allowed Warwick, after Wakefield, to reach London, whence he moved north-west to meet Margaret. He reached St Albans on 12 February, where he paused for four days, enabling his scouts to report on the Queen's line of march. For some reason she turned right after Royston and, passing through Baldock and

Luton, reached Dunstable on the 16th. Learning of this east-west march, Warwick took up a position facing north-west across the two roads leading north from St Albans to Harpenden and Sandridge respectively, his left being near The Cricketers' on the Sandridge road, while on a long extended front reached almost to Harpenden. The line was held by four detached parties, the two left-hand ones covering the two roads running northward. He sent a strong detachment of archers down into the centre of the town.

Margaret decided on a night march to surprise the Yorkists at dawn, an unusual plan in the Middle Ages. She covered the 12 miles down the A5, passing through Redbourne, and veered right into the village of St Michael's. After a slight rest the advance guard crossed the Ver at St Michael's Mill, and moved up Fishpool Street, Romeland and the present George Street. On reaching the little square formed to frame the Eleanor Cross and overlooked by the Clock Tower, the Lancastrians were fired on at close range from where the Boot Inn, the Red Lion, and the Fleur de Lys (where King John of France had been kept for some weeks after being captured at Poitiers in 1356) now stand. The Lancastrians fell back again, having lost many men, to St Michael's, reporting that the town was strongly held. A new plan was arranged whereby a similar advance guard moving out to its left would advance, passing over the then non-existent Verulam Road near the present county hospital, coming down Catherine Street, there to debouch into St Peter's Street opposite Hatfield Road. The Lancastrians had now cut off the strong party of archers in the centre of the town from their main body on the Sandridge Road, thus dividing the Yorkists, but they now had the enemy on both sides. They turned right to meet the archers, and the 1st Battle of St Albans of 1455 was re-enacted. This time the Lancastrians were attacking and not defending.

Warwick quickly heard of the two engagements in the town

and realized that Margaret was now coming from the west,
not from the north-west. Accordingly he altered his whole
main line covering the two main roads by a gigantic left wheel.
He directed his left group to remain almost stationary but to
face due south, and to hold the eastern half of Bernard's
Heath, a shapeless piece of common land astride the two
roads, its southern edge being half a mile north of St Peter's
Church.

The left-centre group of Warwick's army was holding
Beech Bottom, a prehistoric fieldwork built into a natural fold
in the ground before the Roman invasion. In its immediate
vicinity it seems impregnable and Warwick had much
difficulty in persuading his troops to leave the apparent safety
of the earthwork, move up to the high ground on Bernard's
Heath, and thus prolong the line of the left group, which had
now taken up its new position and was eagerly awaiting the
arrival of friends on its right flank. The next group to the
right was more tractable but was much farther away.

Meanwhile round St Peter's Church the Lancastrians had
succeeded in subduing the staunch Yorkist bowmen, who
disintegrated, and the breathless Lancastrians sat down to rest
and eat. They had marched all the previous day and all that
night, had fought two engagements and were fit for little for
some hours. It was mid-day with snow falling before they
could be persuaded to advance and attack the Yorkist position.

Somerset's 9,000 men made a brave show as they cleared
the northern exits of the town near Boroughgate and, advancing in a solid mass, struck terror into the otherwise stalwart
Yorkists, whose left group, covering about 500 yards, was
still without support on its vulnerable right flank; knowing
that its enemy had already won the town, it was very shaky.
Just before the two forces clashed the Yorkists turned their
backs on the Lancastrians and fled down the hill towards
Sandridge.

Up this hill Warwick's centre group, led by the Earl himself, was marching to support the isolated left group, but it was too late. The newcomers, already disgruntled at having to leave what they considered an excellent defensive position, needed little exhortation from the panic-stricken fleeing Yorkists to join them.

The disorganized mass flowed away through Sandridge but Warwick stayed behind, trying to reach the hitherto uncommitted right wing. On reaching it he heard that his Kentish detachment had gone over to the enemy. Rallying the remainder, whose morale had been shaken by mass desertions, he succeeded for a few hours in holding a line some distance north of Beech Bottom. About 5 pm, in the gathering dusk, he extricated 4,000 of his men and, avoiding the Lancastrian army, reached Chipping Norton in Oxfordshire to join young Edward IV. How he managed this remarkable feat or the route he took remains one of the minor mysteries of military history. It seems probable that the Lancastrian army, flushed with victory and tired out, was unwilling to spend another night out in the February cold and let him go.

Why were the Yorkists so shattered? Early in the day their morale was superior to the Lancastrians, tired after their all-night march and the initial rebuff by the Clock Tower. But then the Lancastrians' success round St Peter's Church, a good rest and some food restored their morale, which now equalled the Yorkists'. The morale of the Yorkists' left-hand group dropped gradually when the centre group did not come up on their right. A feeling of isolation was augmented by a feeling of inferiority when the whole Lancastrian army, flushed with its recent minor victory, appeared against them. They could not face it. It was a clear case that when all other conditions are equal, numbers will always tell.

*   *   *

The main battlefield round Bernard's Heath is now so thickly covered with buildings and trees that little of 1461 can be identified. However about 300 yards north of The Cricketers' Inn along the Sandridge Road can be seen, on the left, the last remaining open stretch of Bernard's Heath. Fortunately the highest point of the heath is still open, as a public playground, and there is little doubt that the Yorkist extreme left flank, after its left wheel, rested on the path.

Beech Bottom, now the property of the Old Albanian Rugby Football Club, is easily found near the Ancient Briton on the Harpenden Road. It is a most unsuitable place for a defensive position if the enemy is over the considerable hill to the south, and it is no wonder that Warwick moved forward on to the high ground in front of him. From Bernard's Heath he could not only see the country all round and his enemy as well, but also had room to manoeuvre. He could do very little in or near Beech Bottom.

Towton (1461)

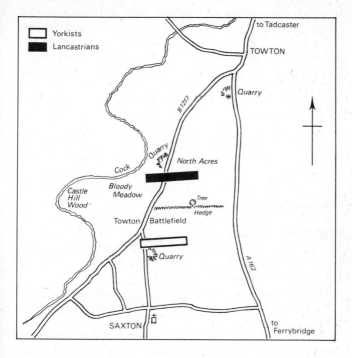

Yorkists

Lancastrians

to Tadcaster

TOWTON

B 1217

Quarry

Quarry

Cock

North Acres

Castle
Hill
Wood

Bloody
Meadow

Tree

Hedge

Towton / Battlefield

Quarry

A 162

SAXTON

to
Ferrybridge

After Queen Margaret's great victories over the Yorkists at
St Albans and Wakefield she had the ball at her feet. Had she
advanced on London, always accustomed to being a prize of
war, she must have found its gates open to her. But she
dawdled for nine days. This allowed Prince Edward to move
from Herefordshire to join Warwick and proclaim himself
King of England.

The Lancastrians marched up to Yorkshire, being joined

by many lukewarm Yorkists in protest at Edward's usurpation of the throne.

Edward and Warwick pursued them to Pontefract, endeavouring to cross the river Aire at Ferrybridge. Here the advance guard, trying to bridge the river, was surprised by a Lancastrian outpost which drove the Yorkists back into Pontefract in great panic. All the Yorkist army stood to and Warwick, anxious to show his men that he at least would not try to escape, drew his sword and somewhat theatrically killed his own horse.

At dawn, with no sign of an enemy attack, the Yorkists forced their way over the bridge, pushing back the Lancastrian rearguard and fighting their way forwards all day to the village of Saxton, where they halted for the night, sleeping on the ground in a hard frost with no shelter. Next morning Margaret's army, now under Somerset, was seen drawn up less than a mile away, astride the two roads, Pontefract–Tadcaster, the modern A162, and Garforth–Tadcaster, the B1217. Her right rested on the river Cocke, the line running along high ground eastwards to the main road, the A162, on which her left rested.

The Yorkists, also on a low ridge, covered precisely the same frontage as their enemy, with flanks resting on the same features.

At 9 am, when the Palm Sunday church bells were ringing, and heavy snow was falling, the two armies advanced simultaneously towards each other. When they were about 300 yards apart the Yorkists halted to fire one volley of heavy-shafted arrows which, aided by the following wind, reached the Lancastrians, causing some casualties. Believing that the Yorkists were nearer than they actually were, the Lancastrians fired several volleys of lighter arrows which, impeded by the wind, fell short by 50 yards. The Yorkists advanced again, salvaged those arrows undamaged by the frozen ground and

fired them back. The archers then closed and a confused fight
with axes, swords, maces and daggers ensued. After a while
the exhausted archers separated and the two main bodies of
infantry advanced, clashing over the dead bodies of the
archers. The two sides were now for the most part locked in
individual combat. Out on the Yorkist left flank in the crook of
the river Cocke is a small hillock, Castle Hill, an extension of
the main ridge on which the Yorkist position originally stood.
Somerset, seeing its tactical value, sent a detachment to hold it
and harass his enemy's left flank. As the Lancastrian superior
numbers were now beginning to tell and they were slowly
pushing forward the Yorkists felt the pressure from the

The battle of Towton

archers on the hillock and there was some wavering among the Yorkist second line.

By about 3 pm the battle was still raging, the men becoming very tired. Despite the cold, their armour made the men perspire and thirst was widespread. During an interval in the fighting one of the senior Lancastrian commanders, Lord Dacres, sat down and, breathless, took off his helmet for a drink. Across the battlefield ran a straggling line of elder trees. In one of them a local youth was hidden, obtaining a grand-stand view of the battle. Being a Yorkist he fired at Dacres, killing him. The lineal descendant of this tree still stands, being marked on the ordnance map at the southern end of North Acres field about 200 yards from the Saxton–Towton road.

At about this time the Duke of Norfolk, who had changed sides in 1455, arrived on the field with several thousand men from his estates in East Anglia, taking post on the Yorkist right flank. The sight of this new fresh threat was too much for the weary Lancastrians, whose morale was never high throughout the campaign when things were not going well. At once they paused, easing off their pressure, and men started to drop out. The most infectious of all diseases, sudden fear, gripped them and the line collapsed. The battle ended in a few minutes.

Many men were drowned in the Cocke, which they found in spate. Many died fighting in Bloody Meadow, low ground in another crook of the little river, which is so similar in position, and name, to that at Evesham. Many bolted for Tadcaster, but Somerset had ordered the bridge there to be destroyed to prevent any such flight and the bridge and banks of the river became choked with bodies. The Yorkist cavalry harried them mercilessly and many were killed before Tadcaster was reached.

*   *   *

To see the battlefield, drive from Saxton to Towton. Three hundred yards after the B1217 comes in from the left the visitor is on the Yorkist front line, by a quarry, whence an excellent view is obtained of the Lancastrian position 500 yards away. Off to the west Castle Hill can be seen but a walk there is not of much value or interest. Two hundred yards down the gradual slope in front an irregular straggling hedge runs across the battlefield, two out of five of the trees being elders. The biggest is probably the descendant of the one that hid Dacres' assailant.

Moving 400 yards farther along the road, and up the corresponding ridge, one finds another quarry on the left of the road. Immediately in front of it the Lancastrian front line ran, and from it an equally good view of the Yorkist line can be obtained. Looking east along this ridge the archers firing at the Yorkists can be visualized, not realizing their enemy was out of range. A short distance behind this second quarry stands the monument to Dacres, although he was killed several hundred yards away. The inscription is almost indecipherable.

Dacres is buried in Saxton churchyard; the gravestone shows vestiges of his coat of arms, carved on the stone on a quartered chequered shield.

The battle of Towton was the biggest battle of the Wars of the Roses, both in numbers and in casualties. The Yorkists had over 30,000 men present, of whom 12,000 were killed or, being wounded, died from exposure on the battlefield that night. The Lancastrians fielded 35,000, of whom 20,000 were killed, the majority during their flight to Tadcaster Bridge after their collapse.

Hexham (1464)

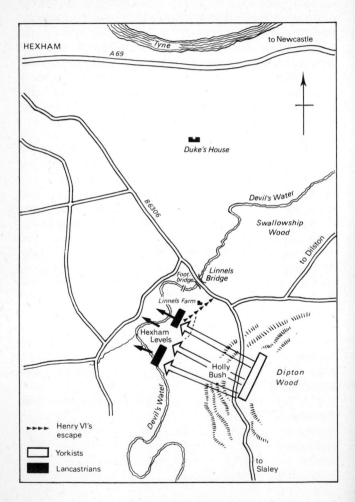

The most confused period of the Wars of the Roses lasted for ten years, starting in 1461 when the Yorkists were defeated at Wakefield and the Lancastrians at Mortimer's Cross. In these ten years young Edward of York, whose father was killed at Wakefield, was to lead an adventurous life. He was to seize the throne, win the Battle of Towton, secretly marry the widow of a Lancastrian knight while the Earl of Warwick, as his ambassador, was in France negotiating a marriage for him with a French princess, be captured by Warwick's retainers, escape to France, return to England, reascend the throne and at once win the Battle of Barnet.

But to return to Mortimer's Cross in 1461. As a result of this victory for the young prince, he marched on London and, slipping past Queen Margaret, dallying after her victory over the Yorkists at St Albans, ascended the throne. Styling himself King Edward IV – Henry VI was in fact still officially King though frequently in the Tower – he began the first half of his reign with vigour.

At once he marched north, chasing Queen Margaret from St Albans as far as Yorkshire, where he inflicted a defeat on the Lancastrians at Towton Moor, the bloodiest battle of all the battles of the Wars of the Roses: the total number killed on both sides was over 30,000.

Queen Margaret escaped after the battle and for three years kept up a desultory struggle in the north of England and Scotland, having the support of some French troops and of course many Scotsmen, who were only too ready to fight against any English army.

This period was one almost of guerrilla warfare. Great castles were besieged, sometimes captured, while others were ignored or the siege lifted. There was much marching and counter-marching, neither side being very anxious to fight another pitched battle, yet all the time looking for formed bodies of the enemy to engage.

Eventually the Yorkists reduced all the great castles in the area round the border, gradually taking the initiative and ascendancy over the not very effective Lancastrian army. The latter, now commanded by the Duke of Somerset with the aged and totally ineffective Henry VI in his camp, felt the Yorkists closing in on them. Somerset fought a minor engagement on 24 April at Hedgeley Moor, was defeated and then withdrew to Hexham. He encamped at Hexham Levels 2 miles south of the town.

Hexham Levels, a flat field about 600 yards square, lies in a steeply sided and heavily wooded valley. Along the western side runs the Devil's Water, a stream 15 yards wide, 2 feet deep, with precipitous banks often 8 feet high.

On 8 May the Yorkists, under the command of Lord Montague, younger brother of the famous Warwick the Kingmaker, appeared on the high ground to the east of the Lancastrian camp on the Levels, slightly north of Holly Bush.

Montague held all the cards. He was on higher ground down which a charge would gather great impetus; his opponent had, behind him, a stream that was probably impassable – certainly a severe obstacle – and he had greatly superior numbers, details of which are unknown.

At once Montague charged, and as might be expected, utterly shattered the Lancastrians in a few minutes. A goodly number escaped, although how or where is difficult to understand. Somerset's camp lay at the head of a peninsula made by two acute bends in the river, and although these bends on both sides of the camp gave protection to both flanks, they also gave the defenders no elbow-room to manoeuvre in at all. The ravine also precluded any withdrawal, or certainly an organized withdrawal.

In its deep and rocky bed the river is today obviously in the same channel as in 1464 and it is clear that few of the fleeing Lancastrians could have escaped with their lives – if closely pursued by the victors. The considerable number that did get away implies that the Yorkists were more interested in plundering the baggage, food and ammunition wagons they captured than they were in improving a military victory.

Somerset was wounded but got away. Later he was captured in a house a mile to the north, near where Duke's House stands today. Vestiges of the foundations of the house of 1464 are still visible. Taken into Hexham he was executed in the market square, and buried somewhere in the grounds of the great abbey.

Two hundred yards upstream from Linnel's Bridge is an ancient footbridge over the ravine. The bridge, about 300

Hexham Levels: Henry VI escaped by galloping along the track in the foreground

years old, doubtless replaced a predecessor of 1464 which Somerset used in his flight to Duke's House.

Henry escaped with a handful of friends. Somehow eluding the Yorkist soldiers he galloped off to the east along the cart-track leading from the Levels up to Linnel's Farm and Linnel's Bridge.

Today Hexham Levels are easy to find. Two miles south-east of the town on the B6306 road (Hexham–Slaley) Linnel's Bridge crosses the ravine of the Devil's Water. Three hundred yards farther on and up a steep hill is a farm road off to the right to Linnel's Farm. Leaving the car there a pleasant walk of a quarter of a mile along the cart-track to the south brings one down to the Levels. On the left is the high ground, Dipton Wood, down which the Yorkists charged. The Devil's Water ravine should be inspected, when its near impassability will be apparent. Although the centuries have worn the ravine deeper now than it was in 1464, it is still obvious what an important effect it had on the battle and what an obstacle it made for the fleeing Lancastrians in the face of the enemy.

Somerset's force, had it been well armed, of good morale and nearly equal in numbers, would have probably repulsed the Yorkists. His flanks secured by the two arms of the ravine, he could, having held the initial downhill charge, have sallied forth from his peninsula, which was well guarded, and ridden into the enemy, perhaps successfully. But his smaller numbers, lower morale and his bad tactical position gave him no chance.

With only a few cows and not a building or a human being in sight, the whole valley of the Levels, and the ravine surrounded by its wooded hills, produces the most peaceful atmosphere imaginable.

Barnet (1471)

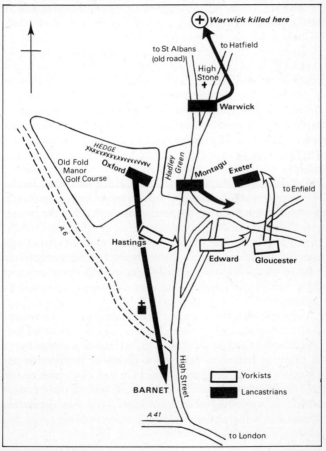

From the Battle of Wakefield in 1461 to the Battle of Barnet in 1471 the monarchy of England, and thus its government, was in complete disarray. England had two kings, one Lancastrian, Henry VI, proclaimed, crowned, deposed and in the Tower, and Edward IV, the head of the House of York, proclaimed king by the peers, bishops and citizens of London.

Despite the defeat of the Yorkists at Wakefield in 1460 and St Albans in 1461, they still held much power in the land and more in London. But Edward remained king for only nine years when he secretly, and very foolishly, married the widow of a Lancastrian knight who had been killed in the Second Battle of St Albans. This understandably infuriated Edward's cousin, Warwick the Kingmaker, who at the time of the wedding was in France negotiating, at Edward's command, a marriage between him and a French princess. On his return his indignation at the very real snub carried him away and he openly collected followers and led an insurrection in the north against the king. Edward's army was defeated at Edgecote, near Banbury, and he sailed for Flanders with his brother, Richard of Gloucester. Henry was taken out of the Tower and replaced unwillingly on his throne again: but six months later Edward excaped from the Continent and, landing in York-shire with some French and Flemish troops, marched to London.

Warwick, now leading the Lancastrians, was at Coventry. Together with Lords Exeter, Oxford and Somerset he fol-lowed Edward at a safe distance, and at Barnet, 12 miles north of London, halted to take up a defensive position to bar Edward's route to the north, where the majority of the people held Yorkist sympathies. He had 15,000 men in three groups astride the modern A1000 (the original A1, before the Barnet bypass was built), and about 300 yards north of the fork road, where the present St Albans Road, the A6, leaves the A1000. On the right was Lord Oxford, whose extreme right lay behind a hedge, which still exists along the right-hand side of the fairway of the third hole of the Old Fold Manor golf course. Today it has gaps, but is quite unmistakable, running along the ridge from the club-house. The stems of some of the main bushes are 8 inches in diameter. Somerset was astride the main road 300 yards north of the fork roads, Warwick himself commanding the left wing out to the east of Hadley Green.

Edward marched out from London with 10,000 men, and was thus in an inferior ratio of two to three against Warwick. Foolishly he formed his line without being able to see his enemy, having arrived after dark.

Edward was one of England's most able kings, and a good general, too, perhaps the best royal general we have had. He had already won the battles of Mortimer's Cross and Towton, was about to win Barnet and, a month later, Tewkesbury. But on this occasion he laid out his troops with no reconnaissance whatsoever – none was possible – and with only the sketchiest idea of where his enemy was. It seems to be the only tactical mistake he made in his four victories.

Edward, in the centre, formed up south of Hadley Green opposite Somerset, 300 yards away, with Gloucester on the right, very near the modern Hadley Wood station and facing Warwick, while Hastings on the left prolonged Edward's left over the main road, the A1000, facing Oxford.

At dawn next day, Easter Sunday, in thick fog, Oxford on the right wing of the Lancastrian army advanced and found the exposed left wing of the Yorkists. Charging, he drove the whole group back in disorder into Barnet town, where they dispersed. Oxford then turned back and, passing through the gap he had made, ran into the rear of Somerset's group in the fog. Mistaking it for Edward's centre he charged and was fired on, both parties suffering casualties. Oxford's men, realizing that their new opponents were on their side, cried 'Treason', a cry that was often heard during the Wars of the

Roses. Many of them simply left the field and the disgust of Oxford's men spread to Somerset's. These, seeing their friends firing at them, also cried 'Treason', and began to trickle away. The Lancastrian line was now in some confusion.

On the Yorkist right Gloucester had made appreciable progress while Edward, in the centre, was keeping up heavy pressure. He then saw that a Cromwell-type cavalry charge would do the trick and he launched a force of some hundred horsemen, his reserve, forward between Somerset and Warwick, to seize the rear. Psychologically it was a superb move and Warwick's army slowly gave way, eventually dissolving entirely. Warwick, still on foot, having foolishly left his horse too far back, tried, in medieval armour, to run into a wood for safety, but was inevitably caught. He was thrown to the ground, his visor prised open, recognized and instantly killed. This most respected, loved and able man, one of the great leaders in English history, had been defeated by the greatest general of his age, Edward IV, now only 21 years old. After dispersing the Lancastrians Edward, now king by *force majeure*, withdrew to Windsor, where he heard of Queen Margaret's landing at Weymouth. He and his army, flushed with the victory of Barnet, marched west to meet her.

Nearly the whole area of the battle is now built over, but Hadley Green itself, the centre of the conflict, is open. It is, however, so limited in size as to be not very interesting. But 300 yards north of the Green stands the High Stone, erected as a battle memorial in 1740, at the fork of the A1000 and the old road to St Albans, with a brief description of the battle. Very near it Oxford must have had his headquarters and his rearward line must have been about 100 yards farther north.

By far the best position to see the only real portion of the battlefield still visible is the third tee on the golf course.

Almost on the crest of the so-called ridge the tee gives an excellent view south, west and north, and of the hedge seen running along the fairway down to the third green. In front of the hedge there are several folds in the ground, which slopes gently down to the present St Albans road, and it makes an excellent defensive position. Had these folds in the ground been held as well as the hedge, and the right flank been protected, Oxford's Lancastrian right wing would have been well advised to stand firm and let the Yorkists take the risk of attacking, uphill, a well-posted enemy.

Tewkesbury (1471)

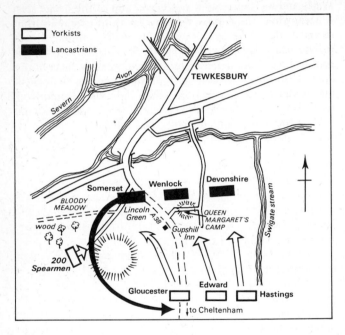

On the day of the battle of Barnet the redoubtable Queen Margaret landed with her son, Prince Edward, the legitimate heir-apparent, at Weymouth. King Edward heard of the landing, and, keeping his army of Barnet intact, moved to Windsor.

The Queen, marching through the West Country collecting an army, intended to move through Wales to the North, there to join her many friends. She left Exeter for Bath and Bristol, where she gathered some artillery, stores and food, and then prepared to make a dash for Gloucester, the first bridge over the Severn, a bridge she must secure if she was going to reach Wales and its recruits to her Lancastrian cause.

Meanwhile Edward had marched from Windsor, his army stronger than Margaret's, with the experience of Barnet behind it and with superior artillery. It also had that potent spur to English soldiers, the repulse and eviction of a landing on English soil. The fact that the landing was by an English queen and her son was of less importance than the landing itself. But she was a foreigner and that was enough.

On 2 May her army, very tired after its 23-mile march from Bristol, arrived at Berkeley, while Edward spent the night at Sodbury Hill. Margaret had done very well. She had evaded the larger army of her opponents, whom she had tricked, and had put 12 miles between them. What a woman!

While in Berkeley she certainly saw Berkeley Castle, and possibly slept there. Her husband's great-great-great-grand-father, Edward II, had been murdered in the castle in 1327, 150 years previously.

Early next day, 3 May, the Lancastrian army left Berkeley to continue its march to Gloucester and the bridge. Two hours later Edward, hearing of the move, started off in pursuit. Messengers came from Edward to warn the governor of Gloucester of the approach of the Queen's army, arrived hotfoot with the news, and asked that the gates of the city be closed. This was done and the Lancastrians were refused permission to enter. Dismayed at this serious setback to her intention to reach Wales, Margaret had no option but to by-pass Gloucester. A further move along the river to Tewkes-bury was the only course open to her; when she reached the town her men were utterly worn out.

Meanwhile Edward marched through Stroud to the little village of Cheltenham and then moved forward to Tredington. Vestiges of the house where the king spent the night could still be seen a few years ago.

Margaret's position lay along a low flat ridge running roughly east and west about a mile south of the town, over which the modern road to Gloucester runs. In the centre of this low ridge lay a large field called the Gastons, now much built over; to the south of it is flat heavy ground through which runs a small stream away through Bloody Meadow to the river Avon and thence to the Severn. Beyond the stream the ground rises again slightly to a distinct ridge on top of which is Stonehouse Farm. To the west of the farm and nearer to the Severn is a wooded rise, known as the Park. Between the ridge and the Park lies a small isolated hill, the Hillock. Tactically the Lancastrian position was sound. It occupied highish ground, with both flanks resting on streams – never a disadvantage – with its front overlooking low ground.

The line was about 700 yards long and was held by perhaps 5,000 men. It was not entrenched. Though the earthwork out on the left front of the position is today called Queen Margaret's Camp it cannot be such. Her headquarters would have been farther back, not in the front line.

Next morning Margaret reviewed her troops as they stood to at dawn and then handed over command to the Duke of Somerset. He, as was customary in those days, also retained the subordinate command of the right wing, while officially young Edward, Prince of Wales, commanded the centre. He was closely supervised by Lord Wenlock, a dubious choice. Wenlock had already changed sides twice, having started his allegiance with the Red Rose of Lancaster at St Albans. He then changed his mind and fought with the White Rose at Towton, and was now back with the Red Rose at Tewkesbury.

Next day the Yorkists left Tredington and marched directly upon Tewkesbury. Edward IV also had three groups, the leading one commanded by Richard, his brother, later Richard III, with himself in the centre and his unreliable brother Clarence, later to be drowned in a 'butt of Malmsey wine', and Lord Hastings in the rear.

When some 700 yards from the Lancastrian position, Edward turned half left and ascended the lesser ridge on which Stonehouse Farm now stands. The whole Yorkist force halted, turned right and faced the three groups of Somerset. The two forces were now only about 400 yards apart.

Somerset had evolved a good tactical plan for the Lancastrians: to outflank Edward's army should it take up the position he expected. Seeing that Richard's left flank, the left flank of the whole White Rose army, was in the air, he ordered Wenlock in the centre to prepare to advance as a subsidiary but very obvious and 'showy' attack against Richard's and Edward's groups in the centre. As soon as he, Wenlock, saw Somerset emerge from cover on the Yorkists' left flank he was to advance.

Somerset then led the whole of his own personal command away to his right and under the cover of the hedges and trees on the Park fetched a great circle round to the west, to come up against Richard's exposed left flank. He climbed the Park, believing he had not been seen, and prepared to come down its eastern face. But Edward had seen the danger of the wooded Park and dispatched 200 spearmen to take post on its southern side and attack Somerset in the flank. At the same time Richard, sensing his danger, turned his group to the left and advanced against Somerset.

Somerset was now faced with pressure on two sides. Now was the time for Wenlock's subsidiary attack to make itself felt and to pin Richard's group to its ground. But it had not moved, and Somerset had to bear the whole weight of Richard's attack and the advance on his outer flank of the spearmen through the wood. It was too much for the great flank attack and it was driven steadily back until it broke altogether. The men became fugitives on the very paths along which they had so recently advanced. Many were driven into Bloody Meadow, whose name leaves no doubt as to what then occurred there.

Somerset managed to escape and, understandably violently angry, galloped up to Wenlock, whom he found sitting on his horse, inactive. Wenlock took the rough side of Somerset's tongue in full spate and his men heard him accused not only of being the cause of the death of many of Somerset's men but also of being a traitor to the queen. Somerset was convinced that Wenlock's failure to advance was yet another example of treachery, and losing all control of himself drew his battle-axe and killed him. Wenlock's men looked on, secretly agreeing with Somerset.

Seeing the defeat and flight of Somerset's division on their right, with their own morale badly shaken by the murder of Wenlock, the centre division turned and fled, soon to be followed by the left. The general advance of King Edward's group in the centre down its ridge after Somerset's defeat undoubtedly demoralized the Lancastrian centre and left, making them waver. Wenlock's murder thus turned the scales.

The retreat of Margaret's army was terrible. Morale shattered, panic rife, the dreaded Yorkists, the victors of Barnet, close on its heels, it was a case of *sauve qui peut*.

Many men were killed trying to cross the Avon by the Abbey Mill, with others drowning. Among them was young Prince Edward, the son of the lawful king, the last of the Lancaster line. He was stabbed by a Yorkist soldier while asking for mercy.

The remnants of Somerset's group, now surrounded in Bloody Meadow and pressed up against the river, were entirely liquidated. Many other fugitives reached the town and sought sanctuary in the abbey and churches; a goodly number eventually escaped. Most of the Lancastrian leaders were killed in the flight, although Somerset did reach the abbey.

He was dragged out and with the few surviving nobles was tried on the spot by a hastily convened court consisting of Richard of Gloucester and the Duke of Norfolk, then, like his current descendant, the Earl Marshal. Naturally all were condemned to death and executed straight away in the market place.

Queen Margaret fled in a carriage, overwrought with grief at the death of her only son, her only child, the rightful heir to the throne. She was captured and thrown into the Tower, where she remained a prisoner for five years. Then her father ransomed her for 50,000 crowns, and she withdrew to France, where she died six years later.

How did this sweeping and improbable defeat for the Lancastrians come about?

The smaller Yorkist army had superior morale based on its recent victory at Barnet. It was led by an active, able young general, King Edward. The latter's skill in resisting Somerset's flank attack was of the first order, and his control of the battle generally marks him as an outstanding soldier of the fifteenth century. It was these two great assets of the Yorkists at Tewkesbury, morale and highly efficient leadership, that defeated the Lancastrians.

The repulse of Somerset's excellently conceived flank attack need not have occurred had Wenlock played his part and attacked when he saw Somerset emerge from the trees on the Park. Had he done so, and thereby kept Richard of Gloucester's group fully committed on its own front, Somerset might well have rolled up King Edward's left flank.

At Tewkesbury there is much to be seen.

The Lancastrian position, or at least its front line, can be fixed to within 30 yards. Running from west to east it crosses the main modern A38 to Gloucester about 50 yards behind and to the north of Gupshill Manor, now a good quality road-house. It was rebuilt in the seventeenth century on the original foundations of the building that was occupied in 1471.

The line then lay along the southern edge of the large housing estate on the Gastons, on the site of the present Manor Place, York Road and Richard Place. Queen Margaret's Camp very obviously could not have been constructed for the battle. It is 80 yards in front of the Lancastrian front line and even if any 'general' had been so tactically ignorant as to build it there, he would have had no time in which to do so. Today the outline turf-covered walls are 2 feet high and at the time of the battle, if it existed then, they were probably nearer 4 feet. There is a strong likelihood that it was built after the battle and was given its present title as a courtesy. Its use, or object, is however quite obscure.

The centre of Richard of Gloucester's division was 200 yards in front of Stonehouse Farm on the present main road. His left was only about 50 yards over the road to the west. From here a broad, gently sloping valley falls away and an excellent fire position facing due west is apparent. But 400 yards beyond the road lies the Hillock. There is little doubt that he sent the modern equivalent of at least one company to hold this hillock, whose summit is only a few feet below his own main position, completely isolated and sticking up like a sore thumb in the otherwise featureless valley. But there is no mention of its being held in any account of the battle and the failure to mention it can be ascribed only to faulty reporting.

Bloody Meadow is of little interest, though the fact that its northern boundary is the river Avon is apparent. Many Lancastrian soldiers escaping the flaying swords or battle-axes of the pursuing Yorkist horsemen must have been drowned in their attempts to swim or perhaps wade across the river.

Tewkesbury Abbey has much to show. The inner side of

the large door leading into the sacristy was refaced with pieces of armour worn by Lancastrians killed in the battle. Many of the pieces are more than 18 inches square, and much thicker than had been anticipated, possibly as much as $\frac{1}{16}$ inch. The weight of a whole suit must have been very great. The door itself is very heavy to swing on its hinges. Behind the high altar and underneath a removable iron grill are a few steep, narrow steps leading down into a tiny vault. The obliging verger will light a candle and there show, immured behind a glass front, the bones of George Duke of Clarence and Isabella Neville his wife. After Tewkesbury Edward IV was

The Hillock, photographed from Richard's extreme left.

firmly on the throne again. He distrusted Clarence and shared this antipathy with the powerful Richard of Gloucester. Clarence had little hope of surviving this combination and was soon executed in the Tower. For some unknown reason his body was brought down to Tewkesbury to be buried and here six years later his widow's body was also laid to rest. Many years later the bodies were exhumed and today the two skulls and the bigger leg and arm bones are clearly visible behind the little glass window.

The town museum has one room solely devoted to the battle. In its centre is a large panorama of the battle but the inaccuracies here are regrettable. The two ridges on which the opposing armies formed up before the battle are barely discernible, the Hillock is not shown and 90 per cent of the two armies are shown in a hand-to-hand mêlée. It is probable that at least half of the men on each side did not come in physical contact with an enemy all day, and the panorama is misleading.

Bosworth (1485)

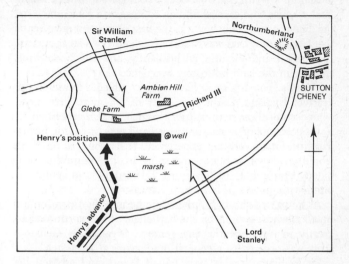

The people believed that Richard III's strength of character would maintain the peace fostered by his brother, the late Edward IV. But many Yorkists began to wonder whether a Lancastrian on the throne would not be better than Richard, and one was available.

Henry Tudor, great-great-grandson of John of Gaunt, was a Lancastrian. When he was 14 years of age, during Edward IV's reign, his mother was advised to get him out of the kingdom. He was clearly the nearest male Lancastrian to the throne and with the Yorkists in full power he was in grave danger. He lived in Brittany until, aged 23, he heard of the death of Edward IV. He was at once invited to England.

Henry landed at Milford Haven with 2,000 French mercenaries, with many Welshmen joining him because of his

Welsh name, and marched into the Midlands. On his way he picked up a youth, David Cecil, a younger son from a minor manor house, and carried him on to Bosworth Field and so to the Tudor court. This boy was the first prominent member of that Cecil family that was to serve England's two great queens, Elizabeth I and Victoria, so brilliantly, and which has been a power in the land politically ever since 1485.

Henry's thoughts must have been troubled. He was in the heart of England, leading an army of not more than 5,000 composed of three nationalities, French, Welsh and English; it was quite unorganized, untrained and poorly led, for Henry had little or no military experience. If he could succeed he would go down in history not only as the vanquisher of a bloody tyrant but, by marrying Edward IV's daughter, as uniting the houses of York and Lancaster.

As he passed through Atherstone he met the two brothers Stanley, whose actions on the battlefield of Bosworth were so greatly to influence the engagement. Meanwhile Richard's army was ordered to a general rendezvous at Leicester.

Sir William Stanley now joined Henry and advised his brother Lord Stanley to do the same. The two Stanleys had met secretly to combine their two forces and next day a considerable number of deserters from Richard's army came in. Henry now had 7,000 men, all imbued with the spirit of liberation from a tyrant.

On 21 August Henry marched on and camped that night 3 miles south-west of Market Bosworth. Richard marched forward from Leicester and camped on 21 August at the village of Sutton Cheney. The two armies were thus about 2½ miles apart.

The king felt supremely confident and the odds certainly seemed to be in his favour. He was much more experienced than his opponent, who had never been in action before. The royal army was composed largely of Englishmen, while Henry had three nationalities under his command. Lastly, Henry's 7,000 were outnumbered by Richard's 8,000.

But Richard was by no means sure how far he could trust his great barons. Both the Stanleys had already shown definite signs of disaffection, while the Earl of Northumberland gave Richard much disquiet.

On the 22nd both armies made for Ambien Hill, a small hillock standing at the end of the low ridge running to the south-west from Sutton Cheney. It was to be the centre of the battlefield and was equidistant from both camps.

Both leaders looked anxiously for the two uncertain Stanley forces, Sir William to the north and Lord Stanley to the south. All four forces were in sight of each other and an extraordinary situation emerged: the two main forces opposite and facing each other were like two football teams, waiting for the referee's whistle. On the two touch-lines stood two considerable groups of spectators, each waiting to see which side was winning before joining in.

Below Ambien Hill and directly in any line of advance by Henry towards the hillock lay a large marsh undiscovered by Henry's 'scurryers'. The battle started in a race for Ambien Hill. The king's scurryers got to the ridge first.

The king's vanguard reached the hillock and, facing south-west, took up a defensive position. The main body, under Richard himself, came up soon afterwards and took post among and behind the units of the vanguard. The rearguard, under Northumberland, was ordered to join as soon as possible and then to face due south.

As Henry neared Ambien Hill his leading units found the marsh to be a considerable obstacle. To prevent his main body from piling up behind it he ordered a sharp left wheel and thus moved due north, only 500 yards from the royal vanguard, which was in its defensive position. Richard's men opened fire.

Presently leading troops of the advance cleared the marsh, following almost exactly the line of the modern railway from Nuneaton to Derby. When its head reached what is now the little railway station of Shenton, Henry's force formed flank to its right and a fire-fight ensued. But the range, although lowered, was still too great for the fire to be very effective.

Richard was now holding 600 yards of the ridge in strength and he began to look behind him for Northumberland to come up and take his place on the left of the line. Richard knew the basic principle of war: concentration.

But Northumberland did not come up and remained just west of Sutton Cheney. From here he could see the two Stanley armies and he did not intend to risk action until they showed their hands. If they intervened on the side of Henry's army – as he suspected they would – Richard could hardly avoid defeat. Northumberland remained a spectator for the whole battle.

Meanwhile, down in the valley, ammunition, as a result of the fire-fight, was running short and a pause in the operations occurred, each side closely watching the other, waiting for it to make the first move. Then almost simultaneously the two armies advanced, the two lines meeting in a head-on collision on the slope of the hill. Today Glebe Farm stands approximately at the centre of the engagement.

Then the Stanleys intervened. Coming from the north and from the south they attacked Richard's two wings. In vain he looked for Northumberland's help, but when this powerful noble failed him he recognized that he might lose the battle, his throne and, in those days, his head. Brave to the last, Richard mounted his horse, collected his bodyguard and rode into the enemy.

Lord Stanley coming up from the south was as unaware of the existence of the marsh as Henry had been an hour earlier. He blundered into it. Richard galloped on down the hill with his efficient, brave, but all too small escort. He, too, ran into the marsh, where his charger was hopelessly bogged down and he himself unseated.

Surrounded by enemy infantrymen who could move only slowly in the marsh when mounted men could not move at all, he was captured, almost isolated and killed. Shakespeare's famous line: 'A horse, a horse, my kingdom for a horse', was probably founded on fact. What other cry would an unseated monarch in the midst of dismounted enemies make?

The battle of Bosworth, *after de Loutherbourg*

When Richard's death was known resistance ceased. His army knew that he was a childless widower and that they fought for him alone. Why be killed for a dead monarch? The royal army melted away as completely as the English army when the only other English king to die in battle perished at Hastings.

There was little pursuit. Henry's enemy had been Richard III – not his army, who were now to become his subjects. A goodly number of Richard's men fled to the north-east – 300 years later a number of relics, arms and so on were found buried in a field to the north of Sutton Cheney.

Lord Stanley was handed Richard's crown, which had been picked up in the marsh, and in full view of the cheering soldiers he placed it on Henry's head, hailing him as King Henry the Seventh.

So the Wars of the Roses ended and the Tudor monarchy began.

The only two physical features that affected the battle are the southward slope of the hill and the marsh below it. Richard's position along the ridge certainly gave him good observation all round. Any attack on him had to come uphill and an advancing body of men on foot would not find it easy going up the slight slope. The armour they wore was heavy and Henry's men had marched along almost non-existent roads, in medieval boots (which had only felt soles) for 15 days. They must have been very tired. The slope of Ambien Hill, meagre though it was, became more and more a factor in Richard's favour.

The marsh at the bottom of the slope, being directly in the way of Henry's advance, was a feature vitally affecting the action. Covering a large section of Richard's front and being almost impenetrable, it should have formed a great protective obstacle guarding a large part of the front and thus allowed

Richard to concentrate farther west and in a greater density. As he, an experienced soldier, did not take advantage of this natural obstacle it seems probable that he was unaware of its existence.

Today the marsh is covered by a wood of 90 acres. A walk in it will soon disclose large batches of coarse reedy grass, such as is often found in boggy ground, or on common land not well drained.

On the northern side of the marsh is a spring, now called Richard's Well, although it is not a well and nothing more than a permanent trickle out of the ground. It never stops flowing and is the cause of the heavy ground in the wood today.

Ambien Hill Farm. Richard's line ran along the line of trees on the left

In any weather the ground is damp all round.

In 1813 a small stone pyramid was erected over the spring where the wet ground starts, and we can safely assume that it is the site of the death of Richard, the last Yorkist King of England.

When Glebe Farm was built in the eighteenth century six cannon balls were dug up on the western end of Ambien Hill. These finds make a pattern. They were fired by Henry's army and show the royalist position along the hill. There is no evidence that Richard had any guns.

The battlefield is best approached from the village of Sutton Cheney, whence a drive of half a mile along the road to Shenton will bring the visitor to the northern slope of Ambien Hill. A walk along the cart-track to Glebe Farm is clearly advisable and the farm is the centre of the battlefield.

Just west of Sutton Cheney and on the road to Shenton is the tumulus where Northumberland waited. It is 5 feet high and clearly defined and from its summit, mounted, he could easily see three-quarters of the battlefield in front of him, including the positions of the two Stanleys. The tumulus is still there.

In Sutton Cheney church is a plaque on the north wall of the nave. It reads:

> Remember before God Richard III, King of
> England, and those who fell at Bosworth
> Field, having kept faith, 22nd August
> 1485. Loyaulté Me Lie.

It was placed in the church by the Richard III Society and is now maintained by them. The society aims to defend Richard's reputation, to prove he did not murder the little princes in the Tower and that he was a good and great king cruelly mishandled by history.

Flodden (1513)

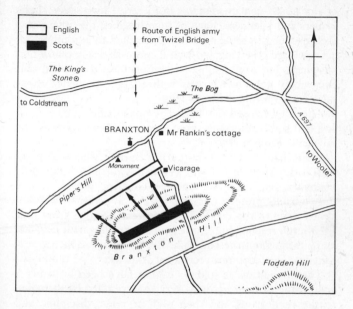

In 1513 Ferdinand of Aragon invaded France, inviting his son-in-law, Henry VIII of England, still happily married to Catherine, to take an army to France and join forces with him. Henry, only 22 years old, 4 years on the throne and youthfully anxious to emerge, was flattered by these attentions by Spain, and took to France a large English army of 25,000 men. The French king, Louis XII, looked round for allies. Clearly Scotland, in the absence of England's main army, might be willing to embarrass her old enemy. James IV of Scotland accepted with alacrity Louis's invitation to invade.

James got together a large army. A figure of 100,000 has

been mentioned, but this is an exaggeration and 50,000 must be nearer the mark. It was alarmingly heterogeneous, made up of almost self-contained races: Borderers, Lowlanders, High-landers and Islanders. Each of them disliked the others, and each declined to serve with or be attached to any other. All acknowledged the king and would enthusiastically follow him anywhere, but would submit to no one else. Louis had sent over 5,000 of his own troops with a large number of Swiss pikes, a new weapon 15 feet long.

The army crossed the Tweed at Coldstream on 22 August and had some quick successes. James sat down to await the inevitable English reaction.

Henry had appointed the Earl of Surrey, who as a young man had fought for Richard III at Bosworth in 1485, to be lieutenant-general of the northern counties, whose primary duty was to protect England against a Scottish invasion. When news of the massing of the great Scottish army near Edinburgh reached him Surrey sent out orders for a *levée-en-masse* throughout the kingdom. By 3 September he had col-lected some 26,000 raw recruits at Alnwick.

Their condition as soldiers cannot have been brilliant. A good many of their 23 days' service were filled by marching to the rendezvous and their skill at arms, discipline and cohesion must have been very meagre. It says much for their patriotism that they were able, at Flodden, to defeat twice their own number.

Surrey was joined by his son, Admiral Howard, who had landed 1,200 marines from his fleet at Newcastle to join his father. Surrey immediately appointed him second-in-command. His army was strong in archers but weak in artillery. It lacked food and supplies generally but it had great morale, and it had the Englishman's best reason of all for fighting, to expel the foreign invader, as Napoleon and Hitler later discovered.

Surrey organized his many contingents into 'county groups'. None of these groups was hampered by any clan system as were the Scots, and men from Manchester had no objection to service with those from Newcastle. The men from York were friends with Lancastrians or soldiers from Preston, and the present-day healthy and friendly rivalry between regiments had its birth at Flodden.

The English moved north-west to Wooler while the Scots occupied the high ground of Flodden Edge, about 8 miles away, facing south. At 5 am on 9 September 1513 the English army left on a 15-mile march north-west to a bridge over a tributary of the Tweed; at 11 am the advance guard started to cross. The whole army then advanced on a wide front, now of course in a southerly direction. The Scots kept the English in close view all day by mounted patrols, but the next day, the 9th, was wet and misty and they lost touch with the English until mounted scouts reported that the enemy had crossed the tributary and were now advancing southwards on a wide front.

James saw that a long ridge behind him, Branxton Ridge, only a mile away, must be occupied. Accordingly he moved his entire army back across the slight dip between the two ridges and occupied an excellent position on the far side of Branxton Ridge, facing north.

At about 1 pm the leading Scottish troops reached their new position, where they formed up in squares, the outer men of which carried the new 15-foot Swiss pikes. Each square was a veritable gigantic hedgehog and when moving was a terrifying formation. Below them they could see the English coming slowly towards them in great groups.

The English advanced until they found one great bog extending across their front with only two crossing-places, one close to and just west of Branxton village, the other three-quarters of a mile farther to the east. Surrey knew of this bog and, finding it more treacherous than he had expected, split

his force into two. The right wing, consisting of the brigades
of Edward Howard, the Constable of England, and of the
admiral himself, crossed by the westerly Branxton ford, while
old Surrey took his brigade, together with those of Stanley
and D'Acre, round to the east crossing.

Surrey and the admiral could now see a lower and less
distinct ridge, running parallel to but short of Branxton
Ridge – known as Pipers Hill, with a shallow valley between
the two. They determined to occupy it.

The negotiation of the bog, the climbing of Pipers Hill and
then the marshalling of the English brigades along that ridge
took two hours, while the Scottish army stood motionless on
its hill. By 4 pm all was ready, and the English stood in four
solid phalanxes. On the right facing the Scotsmen was Edward
Howard, Surrey's eldest son, on the western slope of Pipers
Hill. Next to him, where the battle memorial now stands, was
the admiral, facing a considerable walled farmstead, Branxton
Stead, a little way up the Scots' ridge. Then came the
Constable, while on the far left was old Surrey astride the
Branxton–Wooler road, and just in front of the large walled
vicarage of today. Each of these four formations was opposed
by four similar Scottish formations. In reserve was D'Acre's
cavalry brigade just north of the present church.

At about 5 pm, with rain falling, a mild artillery duel
opened. Its only result was to sting the Borderers, on the
Scottish left flank, into action. They could not stand discipline
or restrictions and after a short while could not contain themselves. They charged forward down their slope until they met
the young recently enlisted men from Cheshire, who turned
and fled.

James had decided to fight where he chose and he had
adopted a defensive position on Branxton Ridge. But the
impetuous charge, without orders, by the Borderers had upset
his plan and had made the remainder of his force very restive.

Seeing the Borderers swinging to attack Howard he ordered his own brigade and that of Montrose, next on his left, forward, down the hill to attack the admiral. The advance was met with a barrage of cannon balls and arrows. But the arrows did little damage and few could penetrate the solid armour worn by the Scots. Indeed Flodden was to see the end of medieval warfare. The bow and arrow was almost finished and the use for armour thereby decreased.

Gradually the two central English brigades were pressed back and the dent thus made in the line reached as far back as the present village street of Branxton, and passed round a cottage now owned by a Mr Rankin.

Meanwhile the Earl of Home's Borderers, flushed with their success against Howard on the English right flank, could have caused immense embarrassment to the admiral and his brigade. But, Borderer-like, they preferred the pursuit of plunder.

D'Acre, with his mounted troops in reserve, had seen the remnants of Howard's brigade streaming back from Pipers Hill and, realizing that a disaster had occurred, galloped forward with 1,500 men to restore the situation and fill the gap. His men dismounted, their horses went back into the steep declivity behind the crest and the cavalry took over the right of the line. The fighting in this part of the field died down.

Three of the four great Scottish groups were now right down Branxton Ridge.

But the fourth Scottish brigade under Argyll and Lennox, Highlanders and Islanders, on the right of the line, had not moved. There it stood, wondering why there was no group in front of it as an enemy. In medieval warfare all soldiers knew that the defence would always be drawn up in the same number of groups as the enemy was deploying in front of it, and each knew that its target was the group matching it. No wonder Lennox and Argyll were puzzled. They wondered whether they should obey orders and await events on their hill – or charge forward and turn the scales in favour of the king and Montrose in the village below.

Stanley's brigade, which was the last to cross the left-hand ford and then take post on the left of the line, was late in coming up. As he came round the eastern exits of Branxton village he saw the stationary, uncommitted Scots group, presumably his target, on the hilltop. He also saw a small re-entrant at this far end of the main ridge, hidden in the trees, leading up to the enemy's flank.

Stanley now showed his tactical skill. Detaching a portion of his force to demonstrate on Lennox's and Argyll's front by a holding attack, entirely engrossing the attention of the Scots to their front, he led in person the remainder, and the majority, of his force round through the trees and up the steep re-entrant. He succeeded in hiding his considerable flank manoeuvre so well that the Scots, with their eyes glued to their front watching the feint attack, knew nothing of his presence on their flank.

Almost at the top of the re-entrant Stanley paused to give his men a 'breather'. After this short rest Stanley gave the word to advance. The archers poured out a deadly fire at 200 yards' range. Then suddenly the fire ceased and the whole of Stanley's force charged. Success was immediate. The Highlanders and Islanders, suffering heavy casualties, turned away to the left from their enemy and, running along the ridge behind the original position, fled from the field.

In the centre of the previously successful advance into Branxton the two brigades of King James IV and Montrose were now being held by those of the admiral, and the Constable and King James sent for the reserves he had left on the far side of his ridge. These charged down the hill but were of little effect, causing the confusion in the village and the cottage gardens to become worse. Stanley saw the confusion far below him in the village but could not see who was having the best of things. One thing, however, he could see: the Scots had their backs to him. Accordingly off he went down-hill at the double, his men, exhilarated by their recent success, close behind him. They crashed into the king's brigade round the present vicarage with devastating effect, almost surrounding it.

At about the same time D'Acre, having nothing to do, moved inward and attacked Montrose's left. This brigade was already wavering and the charge of D'Acre's men turned the scales. Two central Scots columns disintegrated, leaving the field in the gathering darkness. But not King James. He and several of his lords fought on to the end, being eventually killed on the battlefield. Only one of the lords, the Earl of Home, escaped.

The king's body was found next morning among a pile of Scottish dead and was brought into the village church. The exact site the corpse occupied can be accurately pinpointed.

The Scottish casualties were extremely heavy, indeed almost as high as on the opening day of the Battle of the Somme on 1 July 1916 – in each case about 21 per cent of the total attacking force. But whereas there were three men wounded for every one killed on the Somme, at Flodden there were very few wounded who were not dispatched by the English after dark. The English lost about 2,000 men, also a high proportion.

Few battlefields can be more easily viewed than Flodden. A stiff climb from the lane running south-west from Branxton for about 100 yards brings one on to Pipers Hill, the centre of the English position. From here the whole battlefield can be seen and it is unnecessary to move from the simple battle memorial. The Scottish position is formidable and is mostly 200 feet above the English. Had the Scots resisted the temptation to move down their slope and thus forced the English, already tired from much marching, to move uphill, the latter must have had a hard task. But as had so often happened, the indiscipline of the Scots lured them out of their comfortable and strong position.

A few yards from the church, on the main village street, lives the Mr Rankin already referred to. His ancestor, also a Rankin, a Scots soldier, was badly wounded in the battle and left for dead. He recovered next day, crawled to the nearest cottage and was nursed back to health by one of the villagers. He employed himself in burying the dead of both sides. As Branxton is only 3 miles from the Scottish border, the sympathies of the people were much slanted towards the defeated Scotsmen and Rankin quickly settled down, eventually marrying the daughter of his host. His children, his descendants and now the present Mr Rankin have occupied a dwelling, rebuilt several times, on the precise foundations of the 1513 cottage. Mr Rankin shows with pride two metal English cannon-balls found in the marsh behind his house, and three stone ones, fired by Scottish guns. He also owns an iron arrowhead, about 1 foot long and, of course, without its feathers or 'guides'. It must have been a fearsome weapon, for with its weight and at an effective range of 200 yards, would have been capable of penetrating any but the heaviest armour.

The vicarage, a square, imposing, late Georgian building is on a slight rise, where Surrey's brigade stood and was attacked by King James. The visitor can be quite certain that at the gate or by the walls of the garden he is within a few yards of where the troops of Surrey, King James and Lord Stanley met in the chaos of the fight.

Pinkie (1547)

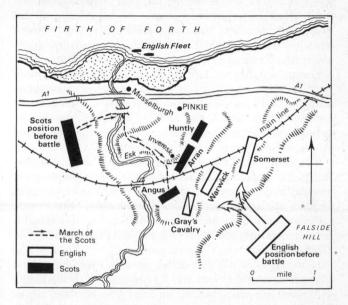

Edward I, perhaps England's greatest king, was the first ruler to see the absurdity of England, Ireland, Scotland and Wales being four separate kingdoms, as well as nations. Seeking to unite England and Scotland, he engineered as a start the betrothal of his son Edward to the grand-daughter of King Alexander III of Scotland, the Maid of Norway and heiress to the Scottish throne. Tragically she died on her way from Norway, and the union of the two countries that would have followed was postponed for 420 years. Other occasions for a union occurred through the centuries, few of which showed much sign of fruition, but one at last seemed very probable, that of 1547.

In that year Henry VIII died, being succeeded by his only son, Edward VI, whose mother was Jane Seymour, Henry's third wife. Henry, anxious as ever to unite England and Scotland by marriage, had concluded a treaty with Scotland whereby young Prince Edward should eventually marry young Mary, Queen of Scots.

Edward's uncle, Sir Edward Seymour, brother of Queen Jane, had been a leading politician during Henry's declining years and on Henry's death managed to have himself declared Protector of the Realm and Duke of Somerset. At once he opened up the question of the marriage of the two young people, Edward being only 10 and Mary only 5.

The Scots were not very enamoured of the union, but seeing that it was some years before the young people could marry agreed to a betrothal. Somerset then started an intrigue to unite the two church parties of Scotland, the French Catholics headed by the Queen Mother, and the English Reformation party, believing that a united Scotland would be willing to bring about the royal marriage.

However, Somerset's meddling in their internal domestic affairs infuriated the Scots and they repudiated the betrothal.

At once Somerset marched an army into Scotland to enforce his will and the marriage treaty that Henry had made – not a very auspicious way to engineer a union between two young people of such tender years who had never met!

Somerset crossed the Tweed with 15,000 men and marched along the coast road towards Edinburgh. From North Berwick onwards he followed the road General Cope was to follow 200 years later, over the Gullane golf course of today, on his way to defeat at Prestonpans in 1745.

The Earl of Arran, the Regent of Scotland during the minority of Mary, was almost a Protestant and had mildly favoured the royal marriage project. But Somerset's invasion of his country was too much for him and he got together a force considerably bigger than the English army. Marching out of Edinburgh he reached Musselburgh and formed up on some high ground just west of the river Esk as it flows through the town, about where the waterworks stand today. It is an excellent defensive position with a deeply channelled river guarding the front, the left resting on the Firth of Forth and the right on a marsh, since vanished. But Arran did not want defence; he needed an aggressive attack to throw the invader back. To defend, with superiority of numbers, against an aggressor is to surrender the initiative, usually an unwise course to take.

Somerset occupied Falside Hill, $2\frac{1}{2}$ miles east of the Scots. Being 400 feet high it completely overlooked the town, the river and the position of the enemy, whose tactical arrangements, and thus strength, were obvious. But the Scots were out of gun range and Somerset moved forward nearly 2 miles to a new position round the then village of Inveresk, occupying a line east of the present maternity hospital. His left rested near Sweethorpe, his right being near Barbachlaw, both private houses.

As Somerset was occupying his new position the Scots, for some unknown reason, abandoned their excellent tactical position and moved forward down to the river, where the mass of the infantry crossed by the narrow Roman bridge, 100 yards long and still standing, which in 1549 carried the London–Edinburgh road, the famous A1. During this move the Scottish army was in great danger. Had it been caught in this narrow defile by accurate gun fire with no room whatever to deploy or disperse it must have been cut to pieces.

However, no action was taken and Arran got the bulk of his army over the river, leaving his cavalry behind on the west bank. He formed up on the low ground where Pinkie House now stands, his left being very near Pinkie Mains, his right near the railway cutting where the A6124 passes over the line.

His abandonment of the excellent defensive position to the west of the river was strenuously opposed by the Earl of Angus, who commanded the Scottish vanguard. He was to cross the Roman bridge first and, on forming up on the new position, to be on the right of the line. His protests were ignored and it was only on pain of treason that he consented to obey orders.

At the start of the battle the left wing of the Scots, under Huntly, moved down towards the shore to come between the English and their ships at anchor opposite the present golf links. They were fired on from the sea, suffered severely and withdrew.

Out on the right the Earl of Angus advanced to occupy Falside Hill. But Somerset, seeing the attempt, sent his cavalry downhill at the gallop to engage Angus, but ran into an unsuspected boggy ditch and lost momentum. However, the cavalry leader collected his men together and started again. But the Scots with their 18-feet-long pikes easily repulsed them, causing heavy casualties and forcing them into a near-panic retreat. In this withdrawal the English cavalry blundered into their centre infantry group, slightly dis-organizing it. But this centre English infantry group under the Earl of Warwick was soon able to move forward to close with Angus who, under pressure, started to withdraw from behind the boggy ditch, at first in good order. Some of the less disciplined Scotsmen, however, stayed behind to plunder the dead and wounded English left by the defeated cavalry charge. Suddenly realizing that they were isolated and that the bulk of Angus's force was now a long way back, they turned and ran to catch up. The Scotsmen in the centre, under Arran himself, seeing the running Highlanders thought they had been defeated, and they too turned and ran. Terror quickly spread all along the line and into the reserve, both of which ran. Somerset advanced with his whole force about

mid-day, and by 6 pm had completely dispersed the whole
Scottish army, which had twice the strength of his own. Many
English soldiers, passing over the ground where their early
cavalry charge had been halted by Angus, saw the dead, and
often mutilated, bodies of their comrades. Such a sight always
infuriates English soldiers, who otherwise are usually com-
passionate to the conquered. They were roused to fury and
12,000 Scotsmen out of the original 25,000 were killed.
Somerset lost only 200 men in the battle. It is almost certain
that many were drowned trying to cross the Esk, as were so

Lord Grey of Wilton's charge at Pinkie

many fleeing Lancastrians at Tewkesbury 66 years previously. The chaos and carnage on the old bridge must have been terrible.

Pinkie is regarded by the Scots as the blackest page in their history, and the anniversary is today known as 'Black Sunday'. It is regarded with some shame, as the Scottish army fled in terror almost before the enemy had struck a single successful blow.

There are two points of interest to be visited at Pinkie. The old Roman bridge over the river Esk at Musselburgh is still very largely as it was in 1547. The main structure of three arches is virtually unchanged. Nowadays only pedestrians use it, although it could just take a small car. The river here is 80 yards wide, flowing between banks never less than 3 feet above water level, while the valley carrying the river is 200 yards wide. Fast flowing and of varying depth, the river still makes a very considerable obstacle. Standing on the old bridge today, observing its narrowness and the severe valley over which it passes, it is easy to visualize the chaos that arose when the panicking Scotsmen fled the field seeking safety over this narrow defile. Had Arran kept behind it he would have been in a virtually impregnable position. Three hundred yards farther north downstream is the modern bridge carrying the present A1.

The other point of interest is the bridge where the road from Inveresk to Carberry Mains crosses over the main Edinburgh–London railway line. Very near this road bridge Angus's right flank rested, the Scottish line running thence north-east through where the present maternity hospital stands. From this fractional high ground, a very gentle, barely perceptible slope falls away south-eastward. At the bottom of this little slope ran the boggy ditch that slowed up Somerset's initial cavalry charge against the Scottish right flank. The line of the ditch is now marked by a meandering, dilapidated low stone wall.

From the bridge and looking east the whole of Pinkie battlefield is in view, with flat, open fields under the plough. In the distance the long ridge of Falside Hill, beyond the battlefield, can be seen.

Bradoc Down, First Battle of Lostwithiel (1642)

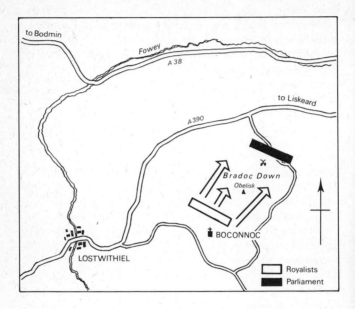

When King Charles set up his standard at Nottingham and virtually declared war against his Parliament, Cornwall was politically split down the middle. The division was not a social one, for the gentry were fairly evenly divided between the two parties. The fact that a man was a tenant of the duchy, and thus a dependant of the king, did not determine his choice of party. Small men usually followed their landlords, who lived among them and greatly influenced their thinking. This close tie between officers and men was outstanding, and in Sir Bevil Grenvile's regiment every man was his tenant or servant. This patriarchal relationship could, and often did, split families among themselves. To pay for this Cornish army the officers had to dip into their pockets, all the men and units being maintained at the officers' expense. Jonathan Rashleigh of Menabilly – the hero of Daphne du Maurier's novel, *The King's General* – gave his silver plate, worth £110, for payment of the men.

On the outbreak of war the two parties put their case before the assizes, which gave their verdict for the king's men; Cornwall became, and remained, Royalist for the rest of the Civil War.

Dorset, however, declared for Parliament, and several great Royalist landowners, among whom was Sir Ralph Hopton, withdrew into the Duchy, taking with them their armed family and estate forces. Hopton took 160 cavalrymen and these formed the nucleus of an Army of the West, which was quickly joined by many Cornishmen.

Parliamentarian supporters retreated from Cornwall into Devon, led by Sir Richard Buller, the ancestor of General Sir Redvers Buller, of Zulu and Boer War notoriety. By November Hopton's army, following Buller, had reached the Tamar; this became a frontier, with the Parliamentarians on the far bank. The two armies were metaphorically facing each other across the water.

The House of Commons, realizing the seriousness of this rebel and efficient army in Cornwall, sent considerable numbers of troops, and money, to the west of England. Hopton, however, despite this growing force against him, carried out several foraging raids into Devon, once reaching Exeter. But his forces, both human and material, were gradually being outweighed by the Parliamentarians and he was compelled to withdraw to the Tamar and then to Launceston, 4 miles inside his frontier. Here his men showed signs of mutiny, due to lack of food and loss of morale caused by retreating. A further retreat to Bodmin followed and here

Hopton heard that two Parliamentary forces had invaded Cornwall. To prevent their junction, he decided to move south-eastward to find the most southerly army, under Colonel Ruthin, and defeat it before it could join up with the other under the Earl of Stamford.

Early on 19 January the Royalists, marching through Lostwithiel with 8,000 men, found the Parliamentarians deployed on Bradoc Down (3 miles east of Lostwithiel on the Lostwithiel–Liskeard A390). Superior in horsemen but inferior in infantry, Ruthin had six guns, although these had not yet come up. He could well afford to await their arrival, having good supplies of arms and food. Hopton, however, was obliged to attack. His army had recovered some of its morale since its withdrawal from the Tamar, and a quick attack might succeed before the enemy's guns appeared. But delay and a possible reverse later might well mean mutiny again.

Ruthin's main army was drawn up at the eastern end of Bradoc Down in full view, about 400 yards south-west of Bradoc church, while his musketeers were concealed by high hedges along the Liskeard road. Hopton posted his six guns on a slight rise just to the west of his enemy's main body. Beside them was the mass of the Cornish army, the pikemen, while cavalry stood on the two wings. He kept a small reserve of musketeers and a few horsemen and infantry out of sight behind his line near Boconnoc, the house of Lord Mohun, one of his subordinates.

Sensibly deciding to attack before Ruthin's guns arrived, Hopton, after ordering prayers to be said at the head of each division, launched his attack in mass. The whole of the infantry charged forward, with the cavalry coming up along both flanks. The redoubtable Sir Bevil Grenvile, though no great soldier like Hopton, was a great man, leading his servants and tenants down a slight slope and up the next on to his enemy's main position. They presented a wild sight, striking terror into the hearts of the Parliamentarians. The cavalry came up on both wings and caught their open flanks. Sudden fear turned the whole Parliamentarian army into a leaderless terrified rabble, and in a few minutes the narrow road back to Liskeard was choked with fugitives; every man ran for himself. The action was over.

Two hundred enemy were killed, with 1,200 prisoners taken. The Parliamentarian guns, which had just arrived, did not fire a shot and were also captured together with all the baggage and ammunition wagons. A very similar result in as short a time was to occur at Prestonpans 100 years later.

The material result of the battle was great, but its psychological result was far greater. Coming so soon after the retreat from the Exeter foray and the Tamar, it put new life into the Cornish army and greatly enhanced Hopton's prestige among his men. It is noteworthy as being the only battle in Cornwall during the Civil War at which Charles was present in person.

The area of the battlefield is now 90 per cent afforested, and there is rarely any visibility of any worth except along narrow lanes, only just motorable, which are little more than rides.

Luckily the last few hundred yards of the Royalists' charge is now a clearing about 150 yards by 300. It is certain that the Parliamentarian front line ran along the front edge where the trees begin again at the top of the clearing. To find this clearing, turn right immediately beyond Bradoc church and then half left at once, down one of the rides. To the right of the second crossride is the clearing. To continue down the ride brings the motorist to a great obelisk clearly marked on the map. It has no connection with the battle whatever, but is useful for orienting oneself in the maze of narrow rides in the large and thickly wooded area.

To drive downhill past the obelisk brings one to Boconnoc

House and the church. Like so many Cornish churches, Boconnoc has a parish but no village. In the little church is the pew of the Mohun family of 1642 – and now of the Fortescue family, the present owners of the house. Charles sat behind a carved oak screen in the family pew at a service the night before the battle, when the text of the Vicar's sermon was 'No Popery'. There is no evidence as to the subsequent career of this brave parson.

Boconnoc House, lying alongside the church, is a stately, dignified eighteenth-century mansion, built on the foundations of the 1642 house.

This is an interesting battlefield, especially in view of the clearing and the church.

Edgehill (1642)

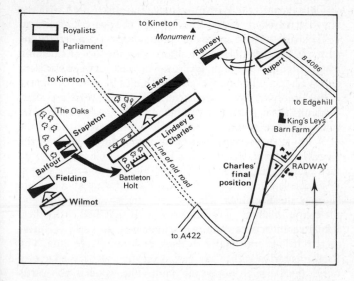

Mutual opposition between the Crown, Charles I and the people, Parliament, had been brewing since 1611 in James I's reign. It was brought to a head when Charles I, copying his father's dictatorial methods, tried to arrest five members of the House of Commons sitting in their Chamber. On finding the five absent he withdrew, and was hooted out of the House by cries of 'Privilege, privilege'. The damage was done, Parliament increased the obstacles placed in the king's way and Charles determined to rule by military force. Accordingly in August he raised his standard at Nottingham, declared war against Parliament and moved to Worcester to join Prince Rupert, his nephew, and thence march on to London to claim his capital.

Parliament's army, led by the Earl of Essex, marched out to meet the Royalist army, but somehow 'lost it' on the borders of Oxfordshire and Worcestershire, and discovered that the king had marched round it and was now the nearer to London.

To shake off the inevitable pursuit that must harass his advance, Charles took up a position along the foot of Edgehill, a long ridge 600 feet high, facing north-west between Banbury and Warwick. The line was about $1\frac{1}{4}$ miles long, with infantry in five groups in the centre, strong forces of cavalry on either flank and Prince Rupert commanding the right wing. The centre infantry group was 100 yards to the west of the village of Radway, the extreme right flank being out beyond King's Leys Barn Farm. The position is good, and Charles's 13,000 men must have presented a formidable sight to Essex's army of 12,000 as it moved out of Kineton to form up about a mile short of the Royalists. The two flanking cavalry groups and the central infantry of each army exactly matched each other. The ground between the two armies was, and still is, intersected by several minor hedges and one large one. The Parliamentarian right flank rested on the southern edge of a wood, the Oaks, an important point. The wood is 300 yards wide and runs back for half a mile.

After an inconclusive mutual bombardment for an hour, the Royalist cavalry on both flanks attacked. Rupert, on the right, moved astride the Knowle End–Kineton road, his left passing within a few yards of King's Leys Barn Farm. The advance started at a trot but broke into a gallop, eventually shattering the Parliamentary left wing, many of whom surrendered, about at the spot where the little brook passes under the Knowle End–Kineton road.

The Royalist cavalry charged on, clearing the still-existing hedges easily as they made for Kineton. Here a few stopped to plunder but the majority galloped on towards Warwick for nearly 2 miles until they met reinforcements coming to support the Roundheads. These latter formed a line and brought the Royalists to a halt. Among these reinforcements was a certain Captain Oliver Cromwell.

Meanwhile the Royalist infantry in the centre advanced for half a mile. As it started, Sir Jacob Astley, its commander, made his famous prayer, 'Oh Lord. Thou knowest how busy I shall be this day. If I forget thee, do thou not forget me. March on, boys.' It cleared the hedges with some difficulty, pushing back some Roundhead groups up their slight ridge. They resisted strongly and soon a stalemate developed. This unimportant little action was witnessed at very close quarters by two little boys, aged 11 and 9, the future Charles II and his brother, James II. Their truancy from the royal head-quarters was discovered and they were hurried back to the safety of Edgehill. James wrote a boyish account of the engagement, which has survived.

As Rupert charged on the right so Lord Wilmot led the Royalist cavalry on the left. Making a big sweep round to the west and then north he pushed Fielden's regiment out beyond the Oaks, and then turned inwards through the wood to attack the Parliamentary right wing. But in the wood were two hidden cavalry regiments. One engaged Wilmot while the other, Balfour's, came out of the wood and, passing round his comrades' right flank, charged the Royalist infantry centre. This he decimated and reached the Royalist gun-park in the wood, Battleton Holt. Having no nails with which to spike the guns, he was reduced to cutting their traces, so rendering them immovable. It is interesting that the site of this Royalist gun-park of 1642 is today occupied by an army ordnance depot, storing gun ammunition. Access is not permitted to the general public.

Balfour withdrew and approached his original position, where he was fired at by his own guns, being mistaken for Royalist cavalry. However, seeing that the Parliamentarian regiments on the right flank were still uncommitted, he mounted another cavalry attack supported by the infantry. At first the Royalists' left flank was pushed back almost into Radway, but their line held. However, the least weakness anywhere might make the whole line collapse and things looked black for Charles. But Rupert intervened. Returning from his charge through, and beyond, Kineton, with his men and horses tired out, he found on the battlefield two exhausted armies. Although the Parliamentarians needed perhaps only one more 'push of pike' for victory, the sight of Rupert's cavalry entering the battlefield deterred them. The King's army still held, a few guns not overrun in the withdrawal to Radway opened fire, and the Parliamentarians paused. Firing died away as darkness fell and in the night they withdrew to Warwick, having failed in their objective of preventing Charles marching on to London. That night Charles slept in King's Leys Barn Farm, now almost in the front line. Of the total 28,000 men engaged, almost 5,000 were killed.

To see the battlefield drive along the Banbury–Warwick A41. Turn left for Kineton after 6 miles. Thence the road will pass on its left within 500 yards of King's Leys Barn Farm, now only a heap of rubble. Another mile on the road crosses a brook, from where can be seen the hedge behind which the Roundheads first formed up. Return through Kineton along the third-class road to Radway. A mile and a quarter along this road brings one alongside the Oaks, 500 yards away, and the road marks the extreme right of the Roundheads' first line. The monument to the battle is on this road, on the edge of Grave Ground Wood, Battleton Holt Wood being 300 yards farther south. It is impossible to reach the Oaks owing to W.D. restrictions. On entering Radway the visitor sees the cottages, or their replacements, against which the Royalist left was pushed, and where they were nearly defeated.

Many relics from the battlefield, mostly lead bullets or small cannon-balls, are in the possession of local farmers. Most have been picked up during ploughing, except a few which have been discovered by a mine detector in the Oaks and Battleton Holt Wood.

To compensate for the necessary restrictions on visitors' movements an excellent view of the whole battlefield can be obtained from the Castle Inn at Ratley Grange, on Edgehill itself. Its imposing tower is believed to have been used by King Charles as his first headquarters and from here he later moved down into the battlefield.

Owing to the necessary W.D. restrictions on movement by civilian visitors within the depot enclosure, Edgehill battle-field must remain one of the very few sites of battles in the British Isles that are disappointing.

Stamford Hill, Stratton (1643)

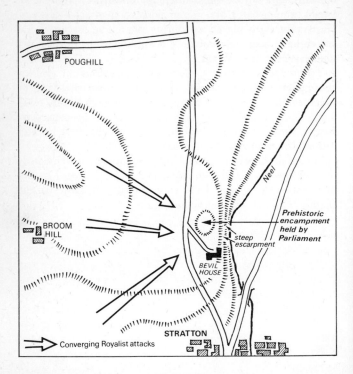

POUGHILL

BROOM
HILL

Neet

Prehistoric
encampment
held by
Parliament

steep
escarpment

BEVIL
HOUSE

STRATTON

➡ Converging Royalist attacks

After Sir Ralph Hopton's great victory at Bradoc Down in January 1643 his army manoeuvred through Cornwall. Hopton's intention was to find the other Parliamentarian force that had invaded the country under the Earl of Stamford and evict it. He reached Saltash in an attempt to capture Plymouth, unsuccessfully, while his enemy lay at Tavistock.

Much marching, counter-marching, seeking, evading and a

veritable game of hide-and-seek ensued in the following months. Minor engagements occurred at Chagford, Modbury and Lifton Down, all inconclusive, but at Okehampton Hopton's army suffered a severe repulse by the Parliamentarians under General Chudleigh and withdrew westward to Launceston, where he gave his men two weeks' rest, a refit and some pay.

Meanwhile Stamford learned from a letter from King Charles, found in Hopton's baggage captured at Okehampton, that Hopton was to march into Somerset with his Cornish army. There he was to join forces with a Royalist army under Prince Maurice, nephew of Charles, and brother of the redoubtable Rupert of the Rhine. Stamford decided to prevent this good strategic move and crossed the Tamar with 6,000 men, marching via Holsworthy to Stratton.

Hopton was now drawing his forces together and at North Petherwin, 5 miles north-west of Launceston, he collected 3,000 men. He marched via Week St Mary and Marhamchurch to Stratton, where he was joined by 1,200 men under Sir Bevil Grenvile.

The Parliamentarians had got to Stratton first, though, and had taken up an excellent position about half a mile to the north of the town on some high ground. To the west it sloped gently towards Bude, but the eastern face of the ridge is very steep, almost precipitous, thickly wooded and quite impassable by cavalry. On the summit of this high ground Stamford had occupied a semicircular, probably prehistoric, earthwork overlooking the western face but open to the east and with a steep escarpment. This earthwork is still plainly seen. It served Stamford well as a fire position but was not of sufficient dimensions to be impregnable.

At 8 am on 16 May the Parliamentary musketeers lined the hedges out in front of the earthwork and soon saw Hopton's army emerge from the area round the manor house where

Broomhill now stands. It advanced up the gradual slope in four columns under Lord Mohun, Hopton, Sir John Berkeley and Sir Bevil Grenvile, each having two guns. Several times the position was charged, the Royalist infantry firing heavily after each rush forward – the embryo of the fire-and-movement tactics of today. Each time they were beaten back by the superiority in numbers of their enemy, and by 3 pm the Royalists were almost exhausted. It was then discovered that only four barrels of powder remained.

Hopton now showed his leadership and ordered his men to lay aside their muskets, thus concealing from them the shortage of powder. He then gave the order to charge right to the top of the hill and the earthwork and carry it by pike and sword only. In Hopton's own words after the battle, 'the soldiers replaced ammunition with courage'. They were irresistible and carried the position, largely by the fear they put into the defending Parliamentarians.

A minor counter-attack, led by General Chudleigh in person, succeeded for a while and in fact surrounded Sir Bevil Grenvile, unseating him. The other three columns, however, converged on the crest of the hill and not only released Sir Bevil and his men but succeeded in capturing General Chudleigh. The Parliamentarians collapsed and retreated in disorder down the escarpment behind them. Hopton immediately held a service on the battlefield to give thanks for the victory. That night the Royalists, now starving, but with high morale, slept in Stratton, where they found large stocks of food and 70 barrels of powder.

The Parliamentarians lost 300 dead and, surprisingly, 1,700 prisoners. Thirteen guns were captured and among the baggage wagons, £5,000, a vast sum in those days. That the defending Parliamentarians, with an excellent defensive position above their assailants and with superior numbers, were defeated and dispersed was a remarkable achievement.

Obviously it was due far more to psychology and morale than to material conditions. Part of this superiority in morale lay in the strong personal link between lord and tenant, between officer and man, in *esprit de corps*.

The hill on which the battle was fought was called thenceforth Stamford Hill after the defeated Parliamentarian Commander. Surely Hopton Hill would have been more appropriate. It is believed to be the only battle in history named after the vanquished general.

As a result of Hopton's military successes in the Civil War Charles made him Earl of Stratton. He died childless but his name is commemorated in Stratton Street, Piccadilly.

This battlefield is easily found. Take the road to Poughill from Stratton and after a quarter of a mile at the top of the hill, on the right, are the entrenchments.

In the centre of the western face a little commemorative archway has been built leading into the Early English encampment. The walls average 6 feet high but there is no moat. The area enclosed is about 100 yards in diameter and to the north, west and south magnificent views can be obtained from this excellent tactical position. To the east the escarpment is much deeper and more precipitous than had been expected and the fleeing Parliamentarian soldiers must have suffered many sprained ankles and heavy falls in their flight. It is only just possible to walk up this great natural bank without going on all fours.

Immediately south of the southern wall is a large early Georgian house, the wall of the camp making the boundary for its drive. The house is aptly called Bevill House, while the biggest hotel in Bude, a mile away, is 'The Grenvile'.

The site of the manor house whence Hopton launched the attack is clearly seen from the road by the little gate leading to the memorial arch. It is a long, steady rise up to the Parliamentary position, and it is surprising that the defenders were unable eventually to stop the Royalists, who must have been badly blown on reaching the top of the rise.

Stratton church is a magnificent thirteenth-century village church. In the churchyard soldiers of both sides were buried but the exact site of the graves is not known. In the north aisle is a showcase with five iron cannon-balls, a rapier and the remains of a wooden bludgeon, all picked up on the battlefield. Outside, and on the north-west corner of the great tower, are the scars of the hits made by some Royalist cannon-balls. Fired at the left wing of the Parliamentarian position, these cannon-balls, with a fraction of oversighting, must have just cleared their target and landed almost at the church door.

Five miles to the north of Stratton is Stowe, the family home of the Grenviles in the seventeenth century. It is now in ruins.

In the author's old home, Trebarfoote Manor, Poundstock, 4 miles from Stratton, were found, 35 years ago, two iron cannon-balls underneath the floorboards of the 'Panelled Room'. The Trebarfootes were ardent Royalists and it is probable that young John Trebarfoote, a teenager in 1643, visiting the scene of the battle next day, brought the two cannon-balls back as souvenirs.

Chalgrove Field (1643)

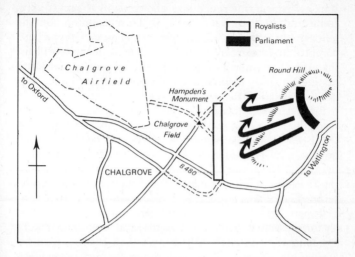

After the Royalist victory in the first major battle of the Civil War, Edgehill, the morale of Charles's army was, of course, high. That of the Parliamentarians was correspondingly low, and for the next eight months the Royalists retained the upper hand.

During the summer of 1643 Essex's army, still suffering from its defeat at Edgehill, with its tail down and riddled with disease, was moving westward from Reading towards Oxford.

Prince Rupert, at Oxford, heard from a Parliamentarian deserter that a convoy from London, carrying £21,000 for the payment of Essex's army, was *en route* for Thame. Setting out to intercept it he missed the convoy, and halted for the night of 17 June at Chinnor. Next morning he moved back towards Oxford after setting fire to his billets.

John Hampden with 200 cavalry was at Watlington. Hearing of Rupert's withdrawal towards Oxford he set off to catch him, perhaps to ride round him, and certainly to prevent him from crossing the river Thame at Chiselhampton. But he failed to catch Rupert who, hearing of the pursuit, turned in a cornfield at Chalgrove to check Hampden. Rupert held his line with the cavalry in front with loaded pistols, and his few hundred infantry behind them, an unusual formation. The position extended for about 800 yards.

Hampden had picked up some of Essex's dragoons, and his whole force now numbering perhaps 350 horsemen rode up the B480 from Watlington. When he reached some high ground near Easington he could see Rupert's 1,200 men drawn up. Despite both the superior morale and numbers of the Royalists he immediately charged them head-on with no reconnaisance and no plan.

Rupert held his fire until the last moment and then a shattering volley from 1,000 pistols and carbines brought Hampden's charge to a halt. Rupert then charged with his entirely undamaged cavalry and drove the Parliamentarians in every direction, utterly dispersing them.

This quite unimportant little cavalry skirmish would barely be known in the history of the Civil War but that Hampden was mortally wounded. He was carried to his wife's house at Pyrton about 4 miles away and died there a few days later. His death was a great blow to the Parliamentary forces and to Parliament itself. He had been one of the five members Charles had tried to arrest in the House of Commons, and with Oliver Cromwell, also an MP, had led the little group of staunch and rigid believers in the sovereignty of the people.

Chalgrove Field is easily found. Take the B480 from Watlington to Stadhampton. After 3 miles do not turn left for

Chalgrove at a big crossroads, but turn right for Warpsgrove. Five hundred yards farther the monument to John Hampden is found at a lesser crossroads. Keep straight on towards Warpsgrove. The new houses on the right are exactly on the line which Rupert took up, his right centre being where the monument, erected in 1843, now stands. Returning, turn left at the monument down a narrow road shown as a cul-de-sac, and after 300 yards the great cornfield across which the charge was made is beyond the hedge on the left. It still grows corn.

On viewing the ground one wonders why Hampden did not attempt to manoeuvre. His only chance against such odds was to 'use ground' and there is some lowish ground on his right flank. This he might have used in an outflanking move, but it is very possible that Rupert's left-flank troops would have seen them. In any case, though, with his vastly inferior numbers he must have been repulsed and dispersed. Hampden's greatest mistake at Chalgrove was to have attacked at all. Though a brave and dedicated man, he was on this occasion a very foolish one.

Chalgrove Field has no natural features that affected the action at all. There is no ditch, no hedge, no stream, no wood, no farmstead which the visitor can examine. But the whole area of the battlefield, 800 yards by 1,000, is so easily found and the charge so easily visualized that it provides an interesting hour.

Roundway Down (1643)

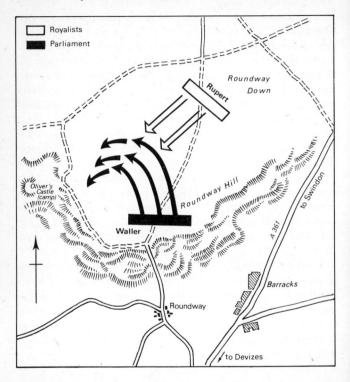

After his defeat and capture at Stratton on 16 May 1643
General Chudleigh joined the Royalist army. Dejected at his
personal misfortune, contemptuous of so many of his men
who had deserted before their defeat, and disliking his chief,
the Earl of Stamford, Chudleigh saw, while a prisoner, the
discipline and morale of the Royalist army. He believed that
a future for a Regular soldier lay in this new allegiance, and

he quickly became of great assistance to Hopton as an adviser and chief of staff.

After Stratton the Parliamentarians withdrew to Devon and Hopton led his army into Somerset, his men united in loyalty to their leader and filled with the enthusiasm of victory.

By 4 June the army had reached Taunton. On its way it had been joined by Prince Maurice and his force at Chard, sent down by the king to meet the men of Cornwall, and the large force of the Marquis of Hertford. The latter, commanding the larger army, merged Hopton's and Maurice's forces into his own and assumed command, a bitter blow to Hopton after his successes. However, he loyally agreed to serve under Hertford and this combined Army of the West now had almost 6,000 men in its ranks, with 16 guns.

It marched north to Chippenham, having several minor skirmishes on the way, and then in a gigantic left wheel encountered the Parliamentarians, under Waller, on the ridge of Lansdown, near Bath. Here they were nearly defeated but the wonderful morale of the Cornish portion of Hertford's army triumphed and they dispersed the enemy. Their losses, however, were very heavy; the most serious was the death of Sir Bevil Grenvile. Grenvile was not a professional soldier but was one by instinct. Worshipped by his soldiers, tenants and servants, he insisted on discipline and by his example, both in battle and in his private and religious life, dominated all around him. His name and reputation are still remembered in Cornwall, especially in the Stratton district where his family home, Stowe, lay in the seventeenth century. He was the grandson of Sir Richard Grenvile of the *Revenge*.

This was not the only Royalist disaster on Lansdown. In the evening after the battle an ammunition wagon blew up, injuring many men and badly burning Hopton who, almost blinded, was unable to take any part in the next few days' operations.

The following day the Royalists withdrew to Chippenham and thence to Devizes, closely followed by the now collected Parliamentarians, still under Waller. The latter quartered his men that night in some ancient entrenchments on Roundway Down, 3 miles outside Devizes.

In the town Hopton was recovering and although quite inactive was able to give orders and, surprisingly, to conduct a parley by letter with Waller on the Down. Waller offered reasonable terms of surrender, which were refused. During the next day Waller's men moved nearer the town, evacuating the old trenches. However, a relieving force of Royalist cavalry, sent down from Oxford by the king, persuaded him to withdraw back to his original position. Hopton, with the cavalry reinforcements, decided to attack Roundway Down next day. On 13 July Waller drew up his army 100 yards out beyond the ancient entrenchments facing Devizes. His foot were in the centre, guns in front of them and his heavy cavalry on the two wings. In front of them was a slight dip in the ground, which rose again to another lesser crest 2,000 yards away. Along this lesser crest the Royalists were drawn up.

Instead of standing firm on his excellent position and forcing his enemy to charge him uphill, Waller foolishly and over-confidently attacked, sending his heavy cuirassiers down his forward slope six deep and riding stirrup to stirrup, apparently the irresistible force. They were too heavily armed, however, to mount the next slope and the charge lost all momentum. Seeing them waver the Royalist cavalry, more lightly equipped and better horsemen, charged down their hill and riding into the by now somewhat disorganized cuirassiers cut them to bits. Utter confusion followed, many riders on both sides being unseated as often by collision as by sword-play.

This rout of Waller's famous cavalry appalled him and as he saw them chased off the field he rode back to his infantry.

Still standing firm by their cannon they were resisting the impetus of the scattered, but victorious, Royalist horsemen. But the notorious Cornish infantry were following their cavalry and the Parliamentarian infantry and gunners, knowing what a formidable force was about to attack them, turned and fled.

The battle of Roundway Down was the destruction of an army. Six hundred Parliamentarians were killed, 900 were captured, and so speedy was their flight that the Royalists found seven guns and all their enemy's stores and ammunition in the old entrenchments. Hopton's prestige, despite his wounds and near-blindness, increased yet again, and after several months of successful campaigning in the west he was made Governor of Bristol and later Master-General of the Ordnance. It is surprising that this obviously efficient and successful general has not a much higher standing in the lists of England's soldiers.

To find Roundway Down take the A361 from Devizes to Swindon. About two miles after passing, on the right, the barracks of the Royal Army Pay Corps, bear left for Calne and the golf club. Three-quarters of a mile along this road is a vague track-junction, clear, yet easily missed. Walk along the left forward track, a 15-foot-wide ride, for 600 yards and one is in the centre of the great cavalry action.

Before this point, however, the site of the earthworks is reached close alongside the ride. These have entirely disappeared under the plough, but owing to the great accuracy of the 2½-inch ordnance survey map (sheet SU06) it is possible to determine their original position to within 20 yards.

The hill down which the Royalist cavalry charged is considerable and after their 600-yard downhill gallop their momentum must have been terrific. The ground is now under cultivation but probably in 1643 was only turf-covered downs. There were no hedges or wire fences and it made perfect cavalry country. The whole field can be seen in its entirety from the spot 600 yards along the ride, which makes a pleasant walk.

On his visit the author picked up a rusty, rigid curved piece of metal from the thick grass on the ride. Its shape, thickness, solidity and size suggest a part of a shattered breastplate.

First Newbury (1643)

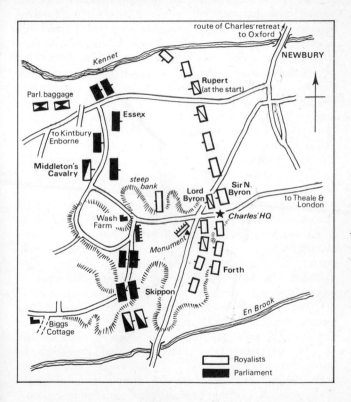

route of Charles' retreat to Oxford

Kennet

NEWBURY

Rupert (at the start)

Parl. baggage

Essex

to Kintbury Enborne

Middleton's Cavalry

steep bank

Lord Byron

Sir N. Byron

to Theale & London

Charles' HQ

Wash Farm

Monument

Forth

Skippon

En Brook

Biggs Cottage

Royalists

Parliament

The tide of Royalist successes flowed strongly through the summer of 1643. Chalgrove Field was followed by Roundway Down and Bristol fell to the Royalists. Charles felt that another attempt to reach London was justified and set off from his siege of Gloucester, which he now abandoned, and marched eastward. Essex had mustered in London some 12,000 men of the Trained Bands – who were but sketchily trained – and had marched to relieve Gloucester. Somehow they missed the Royalist forces, as they had done before Edgehill, and Essex turned back towards London and made for Newbury, a well-known billeting area. The night of 17 October was spent at Swindon, 20 miles from Newbury, while Charles's army slept at Alvescot, 8 miles farther away. A race for Newbury started, in which Prince Rupert by his able cavalry handling delayed the Parliamentarian army at Hungerford. Charles's army slept at Wantage.

The following day, 19 October, the Parliamentary quarter-masters, in those days an administrative advance guard, reached Newbury and were leisurely chalking up doors of houses as billets. Prince Rupert's cavalry galloped into the town, dispersed the escort and captured many of the quarter-masters. Two hours later the main royal troops marched in. They had won the race but Charles, seeing the danger, marched them through the town and down the Andover road. Bearing right after a mile, on to a high plateau – Wash Common – he deployed his army to rest for the night on ground that was certain to play a part in the coming battle next day. His left reached almost to Wash Farm, a large isolated building overlooking the western slopes of the plateau, while the right reached almost to the river Kennet, thus covering the low ground that Essex would probably cross in his advance on Newbury.

Charles, by not allowing his tired army to spend the night in the town, showed that he was a strategist of some capacity. Doubtless he was advised by Rupert. During the night his commissariat commandeered the food collected in the town for Essex's men and sent it out to the troops in the line. The mechanics of breaking bulk, transport, meeting-points, ration parties and guides must all have been similar to the methods used up to the front-line trenches on the Somme, at Ypres and Vimy Ridge, in 1916 and 1917.

Essex spent the night at Enborne 2 miles away. His recently recruited and almost untrained men were footsore, hungry and homesick and were told to sleep out on low-lying damp fields. Their morale was very low and desertion was rife. All ranks feared that the battle tomorrow would be an easy and decisive Royalist victory – no frame of mind in which to enter the battlefield. During the night they moved to a position about a mile short of the Royalist line and in the dark, unseen by Charles's cavalry outposts, managed to get a considerable number of infantry and two light guns up on to the plateau, on to a knoll at the extreme north-west point, Round Hill, overlooking the Royalist line. At dawn these guns opened fire on the Royalists just below them.

At once Rupert was sent to deal with the guns; he brought some of his own guns up to where the Falkland Memorial now stands and an artillery duel developed. Rupert then moved along the high ground and secured a good position near Wash Farm, on the southern flank of Round Hill, while another cavalry regiment assaulted Round Hill from the north-east. In this attack Lucius Cary, Lord Falkland, Charles's Secretary of State, was killed.

Falkland was always a reluctant Royalist. He disliked the king personally, thinking him unreliable, and had unwillingly accepted the office of Secretary of State. He felt very deeply the terrible troubles his country was going through, and believed the minor shortcomings on both sides far too trivial to warrant a civil war. His distress was emotional as well as patriotic and many believed that he sought death deliberately at Newbury.

This attack did not succeed, and an infantry brigade under Lord Byron, ancestor of the celebrated Victorian poet, was ordered forward across the northern slopes of Wash Common.

Along one of the northward-running spurs of the plateau is a
steep bank, some 8 feet high. Byron's infantry paused in its
shelter against the Parliamentarian cannon-balls and were
reluctant to leave its cover, although eventually and half-
heartedly they did so, succeeding in advancing only another
few hundred yards. Something like a deadlock ensued, the
Royalists holding Wash Farm and the Parliamentarians
Round Hill. Both sides now endeavoured unsuccessfully to
outflank their enemy at Wash Farm and Round Hill respectively.

The fortunes of the battle swayed backwards and forwards
and the ground between the two positions became the centre
of a struggle, with one regiment attacking, being halted,

Wash Farm

counter-attacked, driven back, and the roles then being reversed. Both sides had guns and some infantry down on the plain below but no one seems to have sent for them as reinforcements.

At about 5 pm, as darkness was falling, the fighting died down, with both sides exhausted. Ammunition in the king's army was running short and Charles regretfully decided to withdraw from the plateau and retire to Oxford. Essex knew nothing of this move until the morning when, reopening fire with his guns, he received no reply. This entire absence of information about his enemy throughout the night is another example of Essex's poor generalship.

The battlefield of Newbury is easily examined, although a large proportion of it is now covered by a housing estate. Leave the town by the A343 Andover road. About 1½ miles out of the town is the monument to Lord Falkland opposite the Gun Inn, Charles's headquarters. Bear right and less than half a mile on Wash Farm is visible straight ahead. It is by no means difficult for visitors to examine the site. A walk from the lane junction at Wash Farm towards Enborne leads to Round Hill, its height above the remainder of the plateau being barely noticeable. On the return journey to Gun Inn a short divergence to the left down Elizabeth Avenue, on the housing estate, and then left again along the lower arm of Barn Crescent, will bring the visitor to the steep bank, immediately behind a row of garages, where Byron's infantry sheltered. A little farther towards Gun Inn he will pass Falkland Farm, now Falkland Garth, where Falkland's body was brought and in whose grounds local legend says he is buried. This is not so, however. After the battle his family, living at Great Tew, near Banbury, brought the body there for interment. His wife was the daughter of the Great House in Burford and an imposing memorial to him can be seen in Burford parish church today.

Many roads in the housing estate on Wash Common where much of the fighting took place bear names reminiscent of the battle. There are Cary, Essex, Stuart and Battery roads and many local inhabitants know that they live on historic ground.

Second Newbury (1644)

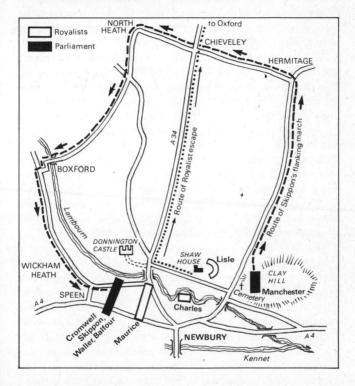

A year after its first battle Newbury was to see another as indecisive as the first, with neither side claiming victory.

In the autumn of 1644 Charles, having three small isolated forces besieged near Basingstoke, Banbury and in Donnington Castle, a mile north of Newbury, resolved to relieve each in turn, starting with Donnington. His approach from the west

threatened the Parliamentarians, who fell back to Reading,
Charles moving to Kingsclere. Next day he marched to
Donnington, where he bivouacked for six days just north of
the town of Newbury astride the present A4 and round Shaw
House, where he had his headquarters.

One Parliamentary army under the Earl of Manchester
marched from Reading and reached Clay Hill, almost half a
mile east of the Royalist position, whence they could see into
the garden of Shaw House and overlook the entire Royalist
line. Not liking the look of it, the Parliamentarians decided on
a great flank march to attack Charles in the rear, a march that
was to cover 13 miles and take 15 hours. Two-thirds of the
attackers formed this out-flanking force while one-third
remained on Clay Hill to 'contain' Charles's army. But somehow Charles got wind of the probable attack on his rear and
detached a considerable portion of his force, under Prince
Maurice, to occupy a position to the west of the village of
Speen, a mile to the west and also on the present A4.

The flank march had started after dark on 26 October and
by 3 pm on the 27th the first pressure was felt by the Speen
detachment. By a previous arrangement the commander of
the flank march, who may have been Cromwell, Skippon or
Balfour, was to fire one cannon as a signal indicating his
imminent attack, whereupon the force left behind on Clay
Hill would advance downhill and attack Shaw House front-
ally. But no signal came and Manchester held his hand.

Despite their fatigue, Skippon's men strongly attacked
Prince Maurice's troops and sent them reeling back through
Speen. Cromwell on the Parliamentary left flank here missed
a great chance, and had he charged with his cavalrymen might
well have routed Maurice's already shaken force. But un-
accountably he did nothing, and the custodian of the now
relieved Donnington Castle was able to harass him, although
at long range, with his guns.

The defeat of the Royalist force at Speen put Charles's whole army in a nasty position. Pushed in from the west and with an obvious threat from Clay Hill on the east, Charles determined on a sound tactical move. He was standing with his two sons, the future Charles II and James II, at his head-quarters in the open field near the present roundabout junction where the A34 joins the A4. From here he ordered Lord Cleveland, commanding his reserve brigade of 800 men, to counter-attack Speen. This attack was immediately successful, pushing the Parliamentarians back some distance and then repelling two rather feeble counter-attacks. Cleveland's skilful handling of his brigade had a tremendous effect on the morale of both sides.

On the eastern end of the battlefield Manchester had at last decided to attack, his delay being occasioned by his belief that the cannonade from Speen was only a desultory fire that had been going on all day, and not the signal he was expecting. Not a very convincing argument.

About 4 pm, as the light was going, Manchester advanced down Clay Hill with 4,000 men, in two converging columns. The Royalist defenders were 1,400 strong, 800 of whom were holding the earthworks of Shaw House and the two flanks, while 400 others were out in front holding a sort of outpost position behind a quickset hedge.

The Parliamentarians advanced in good order, singing psalms, and suffering quite a few casualties with equanimity. They cleared the quickset hedge and some outhouses, but were charged in the flank by Royalist horse as they moved on, being temporarily halted. However, their assailants withdrew into the shelter of Shaw House garden on seeing the large numbers against them, whereupon the Parliamentarians advanced again. But the momentum of their attack had gone and all were held up at close range from the walls of the house and some earthworks on either side of it. A fire-fight ensued during which the Royalist infantry behind their cover caused havoc among their attackers, who clearly wavered and then turned and fled back up Clay Hill. The Shaw House position was held against assault by a minority of almost one to three.

Pressure on the western front at Speen was still severe although the fighting had died down. Charles, after his victory over the Clay Hill attack, rode back to Donnington Castle to see the position. By now it was nearly dark and all he could see was the great number of Cromwell's men still uncommitted. The dawn must bring a renewed attack on him, and he decided to call it a draw and take advantage of the several hours of darkness. The moon was in its first quarter, setting at midnight, and he slipped away with his almost victorious army into the night to Oxford. The defeated Parliamentarians back on Clay Hill, and their comrades in Speen, exhausted by their long all-night march and all-day battle, lay down and slept, quite unaware that in the morning they would find themselves in possession of the field.

Shaw House, now a girls' school, is a magnificent Elizabethan mansion. In one of the upstairs classrooms can be seen a bullet mark, now framed within a brass plaque and proudly shown by the mistresses and the girls. Narrowly missing King Charles as he stood at the window, had the bullet killed him it would have brought the Civil War to an immediate end and saved the lives lost at Naseby.

Out beyond the eastern earthworks are two hedges, between which runs a public footpath. There is little doubt that the quickset hedge held by the Royalist outpost was along the line of these hedges.

Farther to the east and over Long Lane (B4009, Newbury–Hermitage) lies the Newbury municipal cemetery. Across its almost flat ground Manchester's charge passed on its way down from Clay Hill, which is clearly seen 600 yards away. In this cemetery are a dozen or so Imperial War Graves Commission headstones of soldiers who died in hospital in the Second World War. Some of these soldiers belonged to the Royal Fusiliers, a London regiment, and could well have been the descendants of the Parliamentarians in the Trained Bands of London, which fought at Newbury in 1644.

Donnington Castle is well worth a visit with its steep climb up from the car park. Now in ruins, its walls being barely 3 feet high, the gatehouse is still standing and must have given Charles an excellent viewpoint over the western, Speen, half

Shaw House

of the battlefield. Unfortunately a large wood has grown up to the south and west of the considerable hill on which the castle stands and the view in these directions is entirely obscured. The castle is easy to find by driving west from Shaw House and Shaw church to the Newbury–Oxford Road (A34) and crossing over it, then following the lane and direction signs.

The centre of the eastward-facing line was in and around Shaw House, which was a veritable fortress. Around the present tennis courts are three massive earthworks, each about 180 yards long and 5 feet high, forming a precise rectangle. Clearly they were built long before 1644, requiring many hours and many men for their construction. They must have formed an excellent firing position for the defending Royalist infantry who, lying on the three inward-facing banks, must have been almost immovable.

Cropredy Bridge (1644)

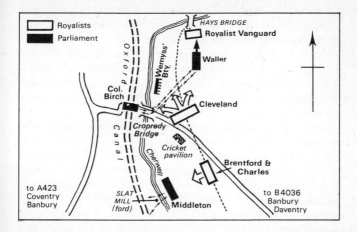

After the inconclusive First Battle of Newbury in September 1643 Charles I withdrew to Oxford. During the winter both he and the Parliamentarian army tried to secure allies, both successfully. Twenty-one thousand Scotsmen crossed the Border to join the Parliamentarian army in the north, a condition of their assistance being that Parliament would openly declare itself Protestant, abolish prelacy and regulate the affairs of the Church of England according to the Scottish Presbyterian model. The king made peace with the Irish rebels, and brought over a considerable contingent. They were, of course, all Roman Catholics, and were thus acceptable to the Royalist army, which was also predominantly Catholic. But the Irish soldiers became very unpopular on account of their behaviour off the battlefield. Indeed after one skirmish against a small force large numbers of them surrendered needlessly and joined the Parliamentarians.

The advent of the Scots across the Border drew many Parliamentarian units to the north to join them, Charles being left in Oxford with the majority of his forces, to manoeuvre against, and usually outwit, the detached Parliamentary units of the Earl of Essex and Sir William Waller.

In May 1644, however, a considerable army had collected against the king, who was by now virtually besieged in Oxford. The Parliamentarians held Abingdon, Witney, Eynsham, Woodstock and Bletchingdon and Charles was in a serious position tactically.

Determined not to be caught within this ring Charles moved out of Oxford, with 5,000 horse and 2,500 infantry, passing near the Trout Inn at Godstow, and thence through Church Handborough to Bourton-on-the-Water. Waller followed him, but Charles doubled back to Woodstock and thence to Banbury, keeping the river Cherwell between himself and Waller's pursuit along the west bank. A small Royalist detachment was sent to hold the bridge at Cropredy as a flank-guard.

Waller knew of a ford at Slat Mill a mile south and sent a force of cavalry to cross there. Having crossed, it rather surprisingly did nothing more. Waller himself attacked the Cropredy bridge in strength with cavalry, infantry and 11 guns. He, too, was successful and drove the Royalist force back from the bridge, where his whole group then established itself on the far side in the large field just north of the bridge. His guns were only just clear of the river bank and about 300 yards to the north, not a good position. The Royalist party withdrew to another bridge, Hays Bridge, a mile north of Cropredy. The Royalist General, Lord Cleveland, now advanced from the east with another strong force of cavalry and attacked Waller, passing over the present very fine cricket field of the Cropredy Cricket Club, scattering the defenders. He captured the cannon together with the officer in charge of the guns, James Wemyss, who had previously commanded

Charles's guns but had defected to the Parliamentarians. The few survivors were forced back over the bridge and through the village, Waller himself barely escaping. The day was the king's. Cleveland's brilliant counter-attack on Waller's bridge-head over the river completely dispersed the enemy and Oxford was safe again.

There can be little doubt that the force that crossed the ford at Slat Mill should have continued its advance and seriously engaged Lord Cleveland. Having captured the bridge Waller would have found elbow-room on the far side either to engage Cleveland or to turn left and engage the Royalists at Hays Bridge. But Cleveland might have brushed aside the Slat Mill foray, and advancing north have attacked Waller's flank and rear as it advanced against Hays Bridge. Waller would then indeed have been between two fires, and equally certainly been defeated.

Take the Oxford–Coventry A423 and 5 miles beyond Banbury turn right for Cropredy village. The bridge is at the far end of the village on the road to Wardington and is quite new, having been built in this century. A small plaque is built into the parapet saying that the first bridge was built in 1314 by the Bishop of Lincoln, of whose diocese Oxford then formed a part. It was much repaired and restored in 1691 and entirely rebuilt in 1937, but on the original site. The fields round are little changed but the river is much narrower than might be expected. The Oxford Canal, which here runs very close to the river, must have taken much of the water, rendering it now only a very minor obstacle to cavalry. Both horsemen and infantry in 1644, however, must have used the bridge. Grave delays in negotiating the probably marshy and certainly wide river bed were inevitable and the possession of the bridge was therefore a dominant and determining factor in the engagement.

Second Lostwithiel (1644)

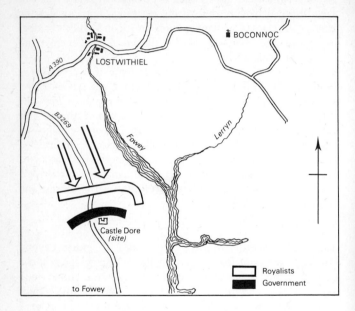

The visitor should not leave Lostwithiel without visiting its other battlefield.

It was a curious battle in that there was very little hand-to-hand fighting except just before the end, though plenty of encirclement, manoeuvre and withdrawals. In the action the defeated Parliamentarians had 6,000 men taken prisoner. They were too many to be kept in captivity and Charles released them after each man had sworn not to fight against him again. Forty-two guns were captured and it was Charles's greatest victory of the Civil War.

After his victory at Cropredy Bridge in June 1644 and

almost two years after the First Battle of Lostwithiel, the king led his army into Devon, which was always predominantly Royalist. Here his army swelled to nearly 16,000 men. The Earl of Essex, certainly the worst general the Parliamentarians had throughout the war, had collected 10,000 men in and around Lostwithiel. Charles moved into Cornwall, reached the area of Lostwithiel and called upon Essex to surrender. Essex played for time, hoping for reinforcements, and so allowed Charles's army to close in on him.

The king set up his headquarters at Boconnoc, in the same village where Hopton had posted his reserve at the battle of 1642. Sir Richard Grenvile, now the baronet after the death of his brother, Bevil, at Lansdown, advanced from Bodmin and stormed Restormel Castle, a mile to the north of Lostwithiel. This virtually impregnable fortress in a crook of the river Fowey, 30 yards wide, was given up by the Parliamentarians without a fight.

A large force of Royalist cavalry and infantry occupied Beacon Hill, and Druids Hill, 1½ miles to the south-east and north-east of the town respectively, while the road to the south was blocked by a Royalist detachment on the river Fowey at Bodinnick near where the ferry now runs across Fowey harbour. Essex was in an appalling position.

Despite a warning to the king by two Parliamentarian deserters that Essex was planning to break out with his cavalry during the night of 1 September, the precautions to stop them were insufficient and 2,000 horsemen got through at 3 am, brushing aside a small party on Bradoc Down on their way eastward towards Liskeard and Plymouth. At the same time the Parliamentarian infantry evacuated the town moving south to Fowey, leaving some time before the Royalist army realized they had gone. Before they left the town they defaced the Great Hall and desecrated the church of Saint Bartholomew, attempting, unsuccessfully, to blow it up.

Their infantry rear-guard under Skippon was quickly harassed by the Royalist cavalry, while the heavy rain made the narrow Lostwithiel–Fowey road almost impassable for the hungry, tired and dispirited Parliamentarians. In the early morning they were being driven from hedge to hedge by the efficient, experienced and trained Cornish infantry and it is surprising that so few were captured.

When about 3 miles short of Fowey the Parliamentarians turned at last and made a stand in the ancient prehistoric entrenchments of Castle Dore, overlooking the roads east to Golant, west to Tywardreath, and south to Fowey and Menabilly. Here they stood from 11 am to nightfall, resisting and repelling the famed Cornish infantry attacks, but after dark, under the long strain, the eastern-facing sector gave way and the Royalists cut the roads to the east and the south. The Parliamentarians were almost surrounded and forced off their line of retreat to Fowey, the ships and escape. The fighting died down for the night.

At dawn the Earl of Essex decided to save himself and with two of his leading subordinates slipped quietly away, without telling Skippon, his next senior in command. Essex wrote later that he thought it 'fit to look after himself'.

This sorry story of defeat and desertion was partly re-deemed by the excellent Skippon himself, who called on his officers and men to cut their way out to Fowey, selling their lives dearly if need be. But the troops had had enough. Exhausted by the strain of the past week and the miseries of the retreat, and now dismayed at their general's desertion, they voted for surrender. Honourable, almost favourable, terms were agreed with the king and on the following day formal capitulation was made in Fowey.

The Parliamentarians, in convoy, were allowed to march back to Lostwithiel, jeered at by the Royalist soldiers who plundered any stragglers or wounded those they could catch.

On arrival in Lostwithiel they received even worse treatment from the townspeople. The latter, doubtless remembering the desecration of their church and Great Hall a few days previously, now got their own back, often stripping some of their late enemies of their clothes, boots and all rations. In the autumn rains, the Parliamentarian soldiers had a wretched time for three days.

The only point of interest today in this major engagement is the prehistoric entrenchments at Castle Dore, lying a few yards to the left of the Lostwithiel–Fowey road, the B3269, just before the crossroads whose arms lead down to Golant, Fowey and Tywardreath respectively. The entrenchment is about 70 yards across and enclosed an early English village, built in the second century BC. The main wall is a steep escarpment frequently still 8 feet high, with a ditch in front, 6 feet deep. On the lower northern side, out beyond the ditch, is a lesser curtain-wall.

The tactical position is excellent and from anywhere along the northern face a clear view of the road from Lostwithiel right up to the entrenchment is obtainable. The walls are now, of course, entirely covered in turf, weeds and a little undergrowth, but are easily seen.

Restormel Castle is a magnificent ruin in a superb position on a steeply sided promontory 300 feet high. On three sides the Fowey flows 30 yards wide, and except from its western landward side the castle must have been virtually inaccessible. As an outpost for Essex's army it could have held out for several days. Its evacuation without a fight is typical of the Parliamentarian morale at this period in the Civil War.

Marston Moor (1644)

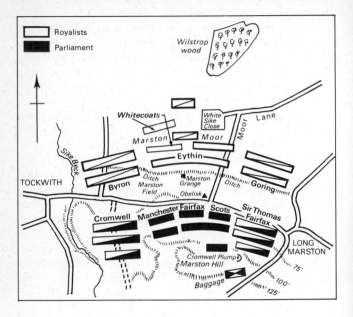

In June 1644, almost two years after the Civil War began, the Parliamentary army had employed a considerable number of Scottish mercenaries as soldiers. They were good but, like most Scottish troops a few hundred years ago, they lacked discipline and cohesion. They were excellent in attack but might panic if things went wrong. They soldiered for the money and preferred to besiege a town or watch an enemy rather than attack. It was less strenuous thus, and equally productive of pay.

In July a large force of Royalist troops was besieged in York by the new Parliamentary general, Fairfax. His total force including the Scottish mercenaries now amounted to 26,000 men. Prince Rupert, with 17,000 men in Lancashire, moved into Yorkshire to relieve the city.

Fairfax decided to break off the siege and the Parliamentary army was ordered to concentrate round the village of Long Marston. Marston Moor is very similar to Sedgemoor. Both have a long, straight cart-track crossing fields so muddy in winter as to be almost impassable. Directly bisecting each battlefield and between the two forces runs or ran a pronounced ditch, at Marston Moor the Ditch, at Sedgemoor the Bussex Rhine. Each ditch played a tactical part in the battle.

The Ditch was, in 1644, of considerable width. There was a hedge running along its south side which formed a useful screen for the Royalist infantry, who were also able to utilize the bank of the Ditch as a firing position. The Royalist Earl of Newcastle saw that the hedge, if defended by his infantry, must throw into some confusion the Parliamentary forces as they advanced to attack his main position about 200 yards farther back. The soundness of this little local tactical plan is as apparent today as it was successful in 1644. About 1,000 men lined the Ditch.

Newcastle had 8,000 men in his main body back from the Ditch, including three battalions of his Whitecoat Regiment, and better infantry did not exist on either side.

Rupert was now supreme commander of the Royalist forces, which totalled 14,000 men, of whom 6,000 were cavalry. He posted a large portion of them on each flank. Lord Goring was in command of the 2,000 cavalry on the left wing.

The Prince's forces occupied $1\frac{1}{2}$ miles and must have presented an imposing sight. The solid phalanx of white-coated infantry in the centre took up over half a mile of frontage, while the two cavalry masses, although numerically smaller, occupied more space. Every man and every horse was in view from the Parliamentarians' grandstand, the ridge running westward from Long Marston, on the forward slope of which they were forming.

The Scots mercenaries occupied the right-centre of the line, the front edge of which was just over the road running east and west between Long Marston and Tockwith. On their left were the two English groups, under Lord Fairfax and the Earl of Manchester. It is impossible to define these two forces in any way other than groups. There was no lower, or sub-ordinate, organization within each group, and the command must have been not only entirely personal but of a dominating and vital strength. On the left of the line was half the cavalry under Cromwell, while that on the right was under Tom Fairfax, 'Fiery Tom', who was to be commander-in-chief at Naseby a year later.

Fairfax had his headquarters on the highest point of the ridge overlooking his right wing. On the summit of the hill stood a clearly defined clump of trees, known now as Crom-well's Plump. It is not known why it bears Cromwell's name. It is at least a mile from where he fought his first engagement. However, the Earl of Leven probably issued his orders there, in which case all his subordinates would have been present when he gave them. The name of 'Leven's Plump' would be more appropriate.

Rupert's troops were the last to complete their concentra-tion and it was 4 pm before he was finally ready. Neither side seemed very anxious to start off. Leven wanted to retain his advantage of higher ground, while Rupert wished to give his men a rest. At 7 pm he decided that nothing would happen that day and ordered the troops' food to be brought up to the front line. He rode off the field to look for a supper for himself. Evidently both forces would get a good night's rest.

But at 7.30 pm the whole of the Parliamentary army suddenly advanced down the hill behind them and, crossing the road, advanced against the Ditch.

On the right flank Tom Fairfax's cavalry crossed the Ditch and moved towards Goring's cavalry. The latter immediately charged, when most of Fairfax's men turned and galloped off the field. Fairfax, however, managed to keep 400 of his best men in hand and, charging again, drove those of Goring's horsemen immediately in front of him off the field too. Pursuing them Fairfax found himself alone with his 400 men, now behind the Royalist main body, wounded and having lost the greater part of his force. Leaving his men, who seem to have been unobserved, he rode back to rally his main body. But he was seen by some of Goring's men and, surrounded, wounded and unhorsed, he found himself alone amid a mass of enemies. Miraculously, he found a horse, remounted and escaped. All that is known is that he removed his white hat-band, the distinguishing badge of the Parliamentarians. He galloped on, picked up his 400 men, passed behind the main body of Newcastle's infantry and, fetching a great circle, joined up with Cromwell's cavalry, which had advanced on the left at the same time as Fairfax's.

Cromwell had at first been held by Rupert's cavalry, and in the process he was wounded; he temporarily handed over command to his subordinate, Leslie, who charged again with the reserve line and drove Rupert's cavalry back. Rupert, leading some of his reserve horsemen from behind Newcastle's main body of infantry, charged into the mêlée. A prolonged fight took place, lasting nearly an hour and with neither side losing or gaining much ground.

When Goring had charged Fairfax's cavalry he had galloped on over the Ditch, for nearly 2 miles. But seeing the Roundheads' baggage wagons drawn up behind Cromwell's Plump his men gave up the pursuit and started to loot the wagons. This incredibly foolish action was exactly copied by Rupert's cavalry at Naseby a year later. Had Goring's men been kept in hand, and used against the right flank of the Parliamentary army, havoc might have been created.

But Goring achieved one tactical advantage in his mad rush forward. A portion of Fairfax's defeated cavalry had in their flight galloped through the right wing of the Scottish mercenaries, putting many to flight. Panic set in and Goring's second line, wheeling to its right, charged the now open flank of Lord Fairfax's large body of foot. This infantry block had now advanced beyond the Ditch and, somewhat isolated, was unable to withstand the cavalry charge; its men, too, panicked and ran. By now there were several thousand Parliamentary soldiers on the run.

An extraordinary tactical position had now developed. By virtue of Goring's successful mounted penetration on the right flank coupled with the defection of so many infantry soldiers, and Cromwell's cavalry's successful assault on the Royalist right flank, the whole battle front had now slewed round like a rugger-scrum.

The daylight was fading but a full moon made some movement possible.

The skill of Cromwell now showed itself. Returning to the left flank with his wound dressed and there finding Tom Fairfax with his gallant 400, and Leslie triumphant after his local victory over Rupert, he decided to lead all the cavalry round behind the Royalist army and attack Goring in the rear.

Goring's men were now well scattered. Some were still trying to penetrate the left flank of the Scots. Others were trickling back from the baggage wagons in no condition to meet a cavalry charge. Cromwell galloped forward and utterly dispersed them.

There was confusion everywhere. Bands of stragglers and fugitives were inextricably mixed; many mounted men had lost their horses and there is no man lost like a cavalryman without his horse. No one knew who was winning. The whole

Cromwell at Marston Moor, *engraved by William French after a painting by Ernest Crofts ARA*

situation was made for a resolute, daring commander and Cromwell yet again was the man for the occasion.

Turning back from this defeat of Goring's cavalry he attacked Newcastle's Whitecoats on their left flank while Manchester's infantry kept up pressure on the Whitecoats' right. It was too much for these hard-tried men. They withdrew slowly to a large enclosure, where, scorning to surrender, they were charged again and again by Cromwell's men. These men were now so elated after their two victories over Rupert early in the fight, and later against Goring, that they went berserk. The Whitecoats were decimated, only 40 surviving. Little is known of the fate of the remainder of the Royalist infantry. The majority, under pressure from Manchester and seeing the Whitecoats slowly forced back by Cromwell's charge, disintegrated, disappearing into the night.

The Battle of Marston Moor was over. In two hours the situation had been transformed from one very favourable to the Royalists with a promise of victory to one where their enemy's cavalry was to defeat them. To two men is the credit due: Tom Fairfax and Oliver Cromwell.

The battlefield of Marston is easily seen from two viewpoints. Leaving the car at the battle memorial on the Long Marston–Tockwith road, a walk of a few hundred yards along a rough cart-track to Cromwell's Plump is worth while. From the top of the hill the whole battlefield can be seen below. Goring's gallop to the baggage train is on one's right. Moor Lane can be directly looked down from the hilltop, leading right to the near-centre of the battlefield. Off to the left the ground over which Cromwell's first advance was made is identifiable. On Cromwell's Plump throughout the battle stood the Reverend Simon Ashe, Chaplain to the Earl of Manchester. He saw the whole battle from this magnificent viewpoint. He left an amusing and mildly interesting account of the battle, but it is rather fanciful and shows no military knowledge. He is one of the few civilians in history who, having seen a great battle taking place below them, have left a description.

The other viewpoint that must not be missed is Moor Lane, 'Bloody Lane', itself. A 200 yards' walk beyond the point

The ditch which the Royalists lined, at Moor Lane

where it crosses the Ditch brings the visitor to the centre of the battlefield.

The Ditch lined by the three Royalist battalions can easily be traced and it is interesting that the sturdy, very long-living, thorn trees are still mostly on the south side of the ditch.

Although it is a rare occurrence, lead bullets are still picked up in the fields that are ploughed. Mr Pemberton, a saddler in the village of Long Marston, showed the author with modest and justifiable pride one culverin ball, three lead musket balls and one lead button, with two holes for the thread from a leather jerkin, all of which had been picked up in the past 30 years.

The father of General Wolfe, of Quebec fame, married in Long Marston church in 1723 Miss Thompson from the Big House in the village. This house is still standing. In it Cromwell slept after the battle.

Naseby (1645)

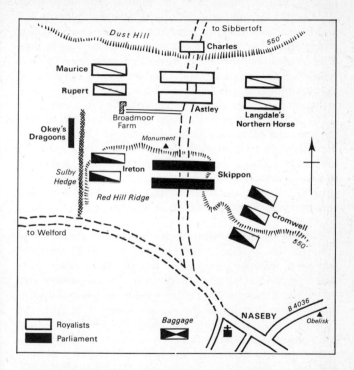

A year after Marston Moor King Charles was with the bulk of his army round Daventry.

On 5 June Fairfax decided to search for the Royalist army near Daventry. He had a completely free hand and his skill as a tactician together with the new discipline in his troops made his army a formidable force. Cromwell was second-in-command, and commanding the cavalry, but the king had no one comparable. His senior general was 66 years old – Rupert, only 25, was becoming more and more independent, while Charles had little military skill. Lastly, the Roundheads had a numerical superiority of nearly two to one. The Royalists' recent capture of Leicester had made them even more contemptuous of their opponents, whom they considered upstarts – their officers included – while the arrival of Cromwell put the New Model Army's confidence high. Both sides felt certain of victory in the obviously impending battle.

On 12 June Fairfax was 8 miles east of Daventry, driving in some royal picquets. The Royalist army in Daventry withdrew to Market Harborough, being followed by Fairfax. In the evening of 13 June the Roundhead main body had reached Guilsborough, while its advance guard had entered a small village 4 miles farther north. There they surprised a Cavalier patrol feasting at an inn, and captured it. The village was Naseby.

The news of this incident reached the king in the middle of the night. He decided at dawn to move out of the town and take up a defensive position. By 6.30 am the position from East Farndon to Oxendon was occupied; facing south it had the village of Naseby and the ridge in front of it in full view. About the same time as the Royalists were occupying the East Farndon ridge, Fairfax moved his main body forward and occupied the Naseby ridge.

At about 7.30 am Fairfax, accompanied by Cromwell, rode forward to reconnoitre the ground. He found the valley between the two ridges very boggy. He considered holding his present position, well down the ridge and covered by the bog, but Cromwell intervened. He pointed out that Rupert, on the Royalist right flank, would almost certainly try to turn the position. It would be better to move the army back up the ridge and so tempt Rupert to attack across the valley, encounter the bog and finally have to charge uphill with his horses blown after negotiating the heavy ground. Cromwell won the argument and Fairfax moved to the ridge behind him.

The area forms a fine site for a battle and is virtually in the centre of England. The stream in the valley flows eastward into the Wash, while only a few hundred yards farther to the west a mere trickle in a ditch runs south-west into the Avon, and thence into the Severn.

As in most battles in the sixteenth and seventeenth centuries, both armies were drawn up with a solid phalanx of infantry in the centre, forming an apparently immovable block.

On the outer flanks was the cavalry, waiting to act as a reserve to come down on the flank or to harass violently an unsuccessful, hesitating or badly organized advance.

Rupert's cavalry was drawn up just to the west of the present Prince Rupert's Farm, while on the Royalist left flank Langdale's cavalry rested on the southern tip of Long Hold Spinney. The whole line covered nearly a mile. Charles's command post was at Dust Hill Farm.

The Parliamentarians were drawn up in similar formation about $1\frac{1}{2}$ miles away. Cromwell's cavalry on the right, owing to a sharp declivity in front of him, was slightly behind the general alignment – which was just behind Red Hill Ridge, though in the view of the Cavaliers.

Out on his left flank, quite separate from his main line, slightly in front of it and facing inwards, Fairfax placed 1,000 dragoons behind Sulby Hedge, under Colonel Okey. It was admirably sited to enfilade Rupert's cavalry when they charged the Roundhead left flank – as they were almost certain to do – but if Rupert went very wide he would take Okey in the flank, or worse still pass behind him. In fact Rupert passed in front of Sulby Hedge.

The Battle of Naseby became the last major battle in British history in which artillery played no part. It became, as did most battles in the Civil War, largely a cavalry battle, the infantry playing their customary, self-sacrificing role as sheet-anchor.

Rupert persuaded Charles to order a general attack. Advancing slightly downhill from Dust Hill and into the depression the Royalist infantry started to ascend the opposite rise. Seeing the advance the Roundheads moved forward to meet it, and the two great masses of infantry were very near to each other.

Rupert felt that he too should now advance when all eyes were on the imminent infantry clash.

Given the order to charge, his horsemen passed outside the two infantry masses but kept inside the Sulby Hedge. From Okey's dragoons there he received a ragged fire which did little damage. Gathering speed as he swept up the gentle slope he crashed into the left of Ireton's line about Red Hill Farm. The sword-fight went in favour of the Cavaliers, whose superior inbred swordsmanship prevailed. Rupert gathered his men together into some sort of formation and resumed his advance, thereby committing one of the great tactical blunders of military history.

He galloped on for a good mile and unexpectedly came across the enemy's baggage wagons parked in a small depression to the west of Naseby village. Rupert had difficulty in withdrawing his troopers from the plunder and it was almost an hour before he reappeared on the main battlefield, where much had been happening in his absence.

Rupert's reputation as a tactician is greatly harmed by this incident. He was serving no useful purpose whatever, and probably lost Charles the battle, his throne and his life.

Meanwhile the Royalist infantry had pushed their opponents back to the crest of their ridge in a retreat that was beginning to have the aspect of a rout. Had Rupert been available with his cavalry to 'improve' this temporary victory the Battle of Naseby would have become a Royal victory in two hours.

Rupert's early attack on Ireton's troops had defeated only half of the Roundheads' left-wing cavalry. The other half with Ireton still in command was intact. Seeing his fellow infantry in the centre hard pressed by the Royalist infantry, Ireton advanced and wheeling to the right came straight into the open flank of Lord Astley's veterans. Okey's dragoons also advanced, joining forces with Ireton, and together they firmly fenced in the Royalist infantry right flank.

Out on the Roundheads' right flank, Cromwell saw the left wing of the Royalist cavalry threading their way through furze bushes and broken country at the bottom of the hill below him. As they started to climb the rather steep rise he ordered his subordinate commander, Major Whalley, to advance with the front rank. The troopers thundered down the hill in superior numbers, and the Royalist horse were swept from the field.

Whalley's men galloped on and almost reached Dust Hill, not far from King Charles's headquarters. There they halted, their horses blown, and took no further important part in the battle.

Cromwell then wheeled his second and third ranks to their left and advanced in waves against the Royalist infantry. They were now beset on three sides and they began to give way. Charles now had his last chance, the timely use of his reserve. But he did nothing and remained in observation on Dust Hill with his reserve for nearly an hour, watching a tragedy being enacted in the valley below him.

The Royalist infantry were practically surrounded, for some of Cromwell's horsemen had passed round to their rear. The regiments of foot laid down their arms one by one, ammunition expended. All had fought on to the end.

During this slow, piecemeal surrender Rupert reappeared

on the field. He would have liked to put in a final charge, but his horses were past it. His feelings must have been bitter as he, a hopeless eye-witness, gazed on the tragedy he had helped to bring about by his rash, pointless and ridiculous attack on the Roundhead baggage wagons.

As the last regiment laid down its arms Fairfax, regrouping his infantry, began to move them forward, through the disarmed Royalists. The king saw that he had lost, turned and rode from the field.

The Royalists lost 4,000 infantrymen almost to a man and their 12 guns that were not used. Their cavalry too suffered heavily, though in lighter proportion. The Parliamentary losses were heavy, especially among Ireton's cavalry and the infantry in the centre, but the total figure is not known.

The battlefield of Naseby seems much changed since 1645. This is but an illusion, however, which is caused by a large number of simple hedges planted when the small fields were enclosed in 1830. Red Hill Farm, Prince Rupert's Farm, Broadmoor Farm and Dust Hill Farm, each a group of buildings occupying a very small area only, have been built since the battle, are comparatively modern and are of no interest to this story. In the seventeenth century isolated farms as such are common today did not exist in this part of England, and all the workers, farmers, labourers, stockmen and so on lived in the nearby village, a very tight little community.

Sulby Hedge still stands as it did in 1645 – for the most part two rows of trees some 20 yards apart growing on turf-covered banks. Towards its northern end it becomes only a single row – and the turf track between the hedges peters out. The steep declivity in front of Cromwell's cavalry is not so considerable as anticipated. The hollow in which Fairfax's baggage laager was hidden is quite clear but is less of a hollow than a falling-back of the ground down towards the western outskirts of the village.

But by far the most interesting things to see at Naseby are in the church. Here is the table round which the Royalist outpost was sitting, feasting, when surprised and captured by the Parliamentarian scouts. For some years it was at the inn, and later removed to the manor house. Here, although treasured for many years, it was eventually discarded and turned out into the yard at the back of the manor, exposed to the snow and rain of many winters. However, the predecessor of the present vicar spotted the table and got permission from the owner of the manor to have it restored. It now stands

Sulby Hedge. Okey's dragoons were behind the hedge on the right

in the north aisle of the church, well worn, but all rot stopped. It is in quite remarkable condition.

Above the table and firmly secured to the wall is a sword picked up on the field and one stirrup iron. The sword has a few inches broken off its blade, doubtless caused in the action. These three relics are naturally very darkly stained with rust – are indeed almost black – but the corroding has been arrested and they too are in remarkable condition.

The parish of Naseby has been fortunate in its present vicar and his predecessor. Both keen amateur historians, they have done much to keep the relics carefully and the atmosphere true. The present incumbent in particular, Mr Mansell, is the most erudite and knowledgeable amateur historian the author has had the privilege of knowing.

Rowton Heath (1645)

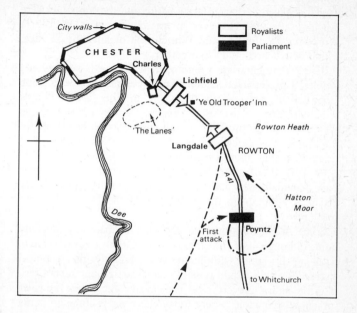

The greatest defeat King Charles's Royalist army suffered in the Civil War was at Naseby. The morale of the New Model Army was very high as a result of its victory, the king had lost most of his infantry and his young general Prince Rupert had unnecessarily surrendered the city of Bristol, and for that reason had been dismissed. The Royalist cause was in low water, and nearly all the military force left to the king was such of his cavalry as had escaped after Naseby, but now without their great leader. Charles withdrew to the West Country around Hereford and Cardiff wondering what to do.

While waiting he heard news of a rising in Scotland under

the Earl of Montrose, and he resolved to march north to join
him. This was indeed a foolish step, as almost all the north of
England was in Parliamentarian hands and the Midlands were
much disaffected. However he marched out of Wales via
Worcester, Wellington and Whitchurch making for Chester,
which he reached on 23 September.

The Parliamentarian commander in the north was Colonel
Poyntz, a professional soldier of much experience, with some
3,000 cavalrymen, about the same number as the king's
remaining army. He closely pressed Charles's horsemen as
they marched up the Whitchurch road but the Royalists got
into Chester as darkness was falling, and Poyntz decided to
do nothing that night, bivouacking at Whitchurch.

At dawn Charles sent his cavalry commander, Sir Marma-
duke Langdale, who had commanded the left Royalist cavalry
group at Naseby, up the west bank of the Dee with 2,000
horsemen.

Some 12 miles up the river a bridge of boats was allegedly
built, although it is difficult to believe that a cavalry force,
with no bridging equipment and certainly no technical
engineering skill, could possibly have carried out such a task
in a few hours. Nevertheless the cavalry got across the river
somehow near Holt, where today the river is some 40 yards
wide and, turning north-east, attacked Poyntz and his infantry
as they advanced from their bivouacs through Hatton Heath
along the modern A41 towards Chester. At first this flank
attack succeeded and Poyntz was compelled to halt and take
up a defensive position between Hatton Heath and Hatton
Lodge, probably off to the left of the road, facing west.
Langdale was forced to withdraw, his position becoming precarious as an additional 300 foot soldiers and 500 cavalry
arrived as reinforcements for Poyntz.

Langdale turned away north across Rowton Moor and made
towards Chester, where Charles, it is claimed, seeing the

moves in the far distance from a command post on the walls, sent out a relief force under Lord Lichfield to help Langdale. Before the two forces could join hands, however, Poyntz attacked Langdale's rear as it moved towards Chester and drove it on and up against Chester's walls, where near chaos developed in the narrow lanes outside the city. Although the Moor was flat and suitable for cavalry action the lanes were certainly not, and the Parliamentary infantrymen had little difficulty in isolating many small parties of Royalist horsemen. They took 800 prisoners, while 600 men were killed or wounded, Lord Lichfield being among the dead. Charles saw the battle on the Moor and in the lanes below him and, realizing he was again defeated as at Naseby, left the last battle he was to fight in the Civil War. He wandered round the Midlands and Wales for 8 months, almost a fugitive, and finally surrendered to a Scots army that had reached Newark. Here he was sent under escort to London, and ultimately to his trial and execution.

Today the lanes are entirely built over, having become a suburb of Chester. It is impossible to get any impression of the battle here, but the visitor should make for Vicar's Lane, Filkins Lane, Swan Lane, Strickland Lane, and there is little doubt that here the Royalist cavalry was decimated.

It seems almost impossible that Charles could in fact have seen the action on Rowton Moor from the walls as alleged. However, from the wall near where Pepper Street penetrates it, he could easily look down on to the Lanes below him and doubtless the legend of him seeing the Battle of Rowton Heath from the walls of Chester really refers to the final disaster enacted in the Lanes below him.

Dunbar (1650)

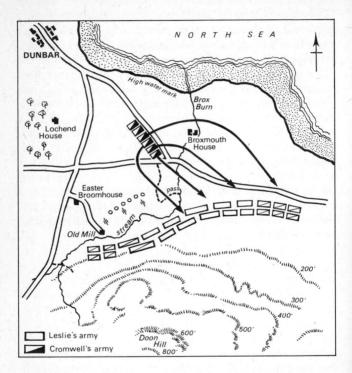

After the execution of King Charles I in 1649 his son Charles was proclaimed King of Scotland. The Marquis of Argyll set about collecting an army to invade England, his prime reason being neither aggression nor the defeat of the English army but to find, defeat and punish Cromwell. The Scots knew he had been responsible for the execution of their king, a Stuart, the head of one of the great clans as well as their sovereign.

The commander of this Scottish army was David Leslie, who had fought under Cromwell at Marston Moor but had now changed sides. His men, 22,000 of them, were almost untrained, mostly with only a few weeks' service, yet they essayed to take on the victors of Marston Moor and Naseby, under a great soldier and leader of men.

Cromwell moved up the north-east coast of England with 12,000 men intending to capture Edinburgh and disperse Leslie's army lined up on Doon Hill 3 miles to the south of Dunbar. From there the Scots could bar the way to the west and Edinburgh, southward to Berwick-on-Tweed, and were in a central position to meet any foray from Dunbar that might be attempted. With almost double the number of his opponents, who had their backs to the sea and little elbow-room, Leslie seemed to hold all the cards.

Next morning Leslie left his excellent waiting position and moved down Doon Hill, northward, to the line of Brox Burn running north-east between the two armies. Here an English outpost was captured in an isolated farm near where today the A1 crosses the Burn. Cromwell went forward to reconnoitre from Broxmouth House and there saw that while Leslie's left was protected by the almost impassable Brox Burn, his right was on open level ground very suited to cavalry action. He decided to attack at dawn next day.

At about 4 am a brigade of horse led off supported by two infantry regiments, and the Burn was crossed in the right centre of the Scottish line astride the Dunbar–Berwick road. Although surprised by the dawn attack, the Scots fought well, but Lambert's English brigade got across the Burn and precariously held the south bank. A mounted Scottish counter-attack drove the English back slightly, but an attack in the centre by Monk's brigade, doubtless containing the Coldstream Guards, held the attention of Leslie and the Scots. The two lines, now in close contact, became locked together.

Then, as usual, Cromwell's skill as a cavalry leader came to the fore. Moving due east with his own regiment of horse, and a brigade of infantry, he passed round to the far side of Broxmouth House lying between the present A1 and the sea and fetched a great circle round to the south. He hoped to deliver the blow that was to decide the day, and he was right. Wheeling right he charged the extreme right wing of the Scots, who resisted valiantly. Their colonel, a Campbell, was killed by a sergeant of Cromwell's regiment, and the infantry came on to clinch the matter.

Leslie's right wing disintegrated, the cavalry galloping off to Berwick or Haddington. The Scottish infantry in the centre resisted stiffly but those on the two flanks gave way and either surrendered or fled. The battle was over. The sun was now appearing over the horizon and in this hour and a half, Cromwell's leadership and his superb army had utterly defeated a Scottish army of twice its size, defending its own country against the invader. They lost 3,000 killed and 10,000 prisoners, most of whom, being wounded, were released. Thirty guns were captured and 200 colours, while Cromwell claimed that he lost only 30 men. It was, perhaps, the finest example of his tactical skill, dominance and leadership.

A little monument has been erected on the A1 by a bus shelter at the entrance to the Portland Cement Works. It is 300 yards behind the site of where Leslie's right-hand regiment stood and where Cromwell's cavalry and infantry flank attack came in.

Moving north-west along the A1 a little turning to the left to Pinkerton Hill should be taken. After crossing over the main railway line, and proceeding another 300 yards to where a cart-track leads off to Little Pinkerton, the visitor is in the centre of Leslie's line. Cromwell's cavalry charge caught the

Scots' unprotected right flank about where the railway bridge (just crossed) now stands. The woods round Broxmouth Ward and to the west of the bridge did not exist in 1650. Back on to the main A1 and moving north-west again, the visitor will come to the fork where the main road goes off due west to Haddington and the northward road to Dunbar. In the angle between the two roads Cromwell's army formed up and from here parts of it moved down to the Brox Burn in the initial attack. Here Cromwell's own flank-move started.

A visit to Easter Broomhouse to the left, off the Haddington road, and beyond it to the Old Mill is worth while, as the Brox Burn is seen in its ravine and across it the Scottish position and, in the distance, Doon Hill. The ravine, frequently 100 yards wide, lies in one of the most picturesque rural, wooded and utterly quiet valleys the author has ever visited.

Worcester (1651)

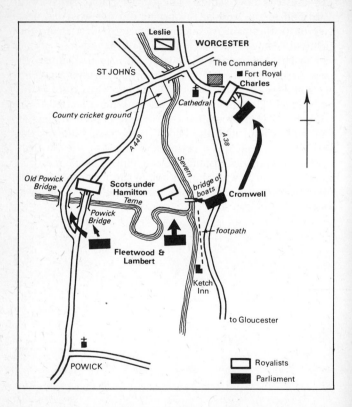

After the Second Battle of Newbury the king's two sons, Charles, Prince of Wales, and his younger brother James, were sent to Holland to live almost in exile. Immediately after the execution of his father in 1649 young Charles was proclaimed Charles II, King of Scotland, and invited to return and claim his throne. He landed in Scotland in June 1650, where he was proclaimed king at Edinburgh amid great rejoicing.

Cromwell, now the dictator of England, was determined to prevent the establishment of a monarchy in Scotland and believed that the country should share in the fortunes of a republic. Accordingly he marched into Scotland with 16,000 men and utterly defeated the Scots at Dunbar. Despite their defeat and determined not to accept republicanism, the Scots crowned Charles at Scone, where he quickly raised an army of 16,000. Many of those who had escaped from Dunbar were in the new army and were anxious both to avenge their defeat and to expel the English, now in and around Edinburgh. Charles, however, decided to avoid an encounter, and with his untrained but enthusiastic army slipped between Edinburgh and Glasgow and entered England at Carlisle, where he was proclaimed King of England on English soil by Englishmen. He marched on hurriedly and in three weeks was in the city of Worcester. His reason for diverging from the direct route to his capital, London, was to draw the Welsh from their mountains to join his army, but they proved unenthusiastic.

Cromwell followed at once, his cavalry under General Lambert, covering 200 miles in four days. He ordered all detached forces no matter how small to concentrate at Coventry, there to await his arrival. The Parliamentary army began to close in, and by 24 August they were astride the main road from Worcester to London with 30,000 men. Charles's position was now very serious. His army, despite a few recruits from Wales, was no stronger than its original size and he knew that Cromwell had outlying contingents coming in. Time was on Cromwell's side and he deliberately blocked the way to the south, towards London, and to the west into Wales.

At Worcester the river Severn runs north and south with the city on the eastern bank. Two miles to the south a considerable tributary joins it from the west, the river Teme, 30 yards wide and with banks 10 feet high. The Teme is crossed by a bridge at Powick, a mile and a half before it joins the Severn, across which there was, and is, no bridge for 8 miles below the city.

Next day, 3 September, was the anniversary of the Battle of Dunbar, where the Scots had been decisively beaten the previous year. No doubt this fact depressed Charles's men, 80 per cent of whom were Scotsmen.

The only crossing of the unfordable Severn and Teme was at Powick, presenting a grave problem to Cromwell. Accordingly he ordered General Fleetwood to cross the Severn at Upton, 9 miles south of Worcester, and there commandeer some large flat-bottomed boats and tow them upstream to near the junction of the two rivers. It must have been a gigantic task as the Severn here is fast and runs between deep and steep banks. Fleetwood was given 11,000 men and of course all the towing was done by man-power. One pontoon bridge was to be built across both rivers. The entire absence of opposition by the Scottish troops lying in the meadows between the two rivers seems quite extraordinary.

A Royalist outpost across the river Teme was holding the village of Powick half a mile to the south of the bridge and there for a brief while held up the advancing Parliamentarians, who were to force the crossing of Powick bridge. The brief engagement in the churchyard has left bullet marks on the base of the church tower, which can be clearly seen.

From the Royalist outpost Fleetwood's men as they withdrew came up to Powick Bridge, but owing to the damage only infantry could cross, the mounted men having to find the ford a mile farther upstream.

Meanwhile the towed boats had arrived near the junction.

Five boats went up the Teme for 100 yards and there the pontoon bridge was started, while 15 boats went a similar distance up the Severn. The two bridge-heads were secured to protect the building by men ferried over in small rowing boats to keep at bay any Royalist patrols. They were seen by one patrol which gave the alarm, and reinforcements were sent from the city, but the two bridges were completed with little opposition: an astonishing fact. Cromwell led his men over the newly built Severn bridge, joining forces with General Lambert, who had by now also crossed the Teme. They advanced together and gradually pushed back the considerable Royalist infantry force in the meadows between the two rivers.

Meanwhile, from the cathedral tower Charles not only saw the strong advance across the meadows below him, but also noticed that Cromwell's right wing was becoming isolated. It had the unfordable Severn between it and Cromwell's main operation and was clearly vulnerable. Accordingly he collected all the horsemen he could find – one Scottish cavalry regiment, Leslie's, refused to co-operate – and led them through the East Gate, now the Sidbury, against the slowly advancing Parliamentarian right wing. The Royalists quickly threw them back in disorder and moved on to secure a good position on Red Hill, now a housing estate astride the Worcester–Pershore Road, the A44.

It was a critical moment but Oliver Cromwell showed his genius as a leader of men, as he had done at Marston Moor. Leaving Fleetwood in command in the meadows, to keep up the pressure, he galloped back over his pontoon bridge, followed by his successful brigade and, picking up his retreating right wing, led them back and counter-attacked the Royalists on Red Hill with all his strength. His leadership and iron will prevailed and the Scots were pushed back off the hill and, indeed, back through the Sidbury and into the city.

The Scots refused to stand, and although Charles rode up and down exhorting them, he could not hold them and many threw down their arms and drifted away through the city, led by Leslie's horse. Meanwhile Fleetwood's advance across the meadows between the two rivers gathered momentum, and his force eventually pushed the Scots back to, and across, the present county cricket ground. Here the permanent bridge over the Severn was secured and all chance of Charles's army escaping to the west vanished.

Charles's English cavalry now stood fast, and to secure his escape charged back down the High Street and then the Sidbury. Held and then forced back they reached the town hall, where a last-ditch stand was made: they were eventually overcome. In the dusk Charles escaped to Boscobel Oak and after several weeks of hairbreadth adventures he reached Shoreham Harbour and a boat for France. This famous oak today is commemorated by over 400 English public houses called the 'Royal Oak'.

Cromwell regarded his victory at Worcester as 'God's crowning mercy'. Certainly England was not again to be threatened by an army, Stuart or otherwise, until Monmouth's abortive adventure over 30 years later, which ended at Sedgemoor.

To visit the site of the Battle of Worcester drive up the A4021 from Upton to Powick to see the churchyard where the outpost skirmish took place, and the bullet marks on the base of the church tower. Drive on towards Worcester, crossing the Teme by the modern bridge. Two hundred yards across the meadow to the left the old bridge is reached, clearly showing portions of the original bridge before the partial rebuilding in 1837. If you drive on, the meadows up to the county cricket ground are on the right.

Leave Worcester by the Pershore road, the A44, down the Sidbury. On the left of the road immediately opposite the turning to Kempsey is the Commandery, a building already standing in 1651. It was the headquarters of the Royalist forces defending the East Gate, and here Charles collected the troops to attack Cromwell's temporarily weak right flank. It is a magnificent example of a sixteenth-century county town 'big house'. The main hall and the formal staircase are superb, while the rooms upstairs should not be missed. After the battle many wounded from both sides were brought into the house.

Drive on down the A44 to the Ketch Inn. A walk back along the river bank for 500 yards brings one to where Cromwell's pontoon bridge was erected. The site of Fleetwood's bridge can be seen 300 yards away, across the confluence.

Sedgemoor (1685)

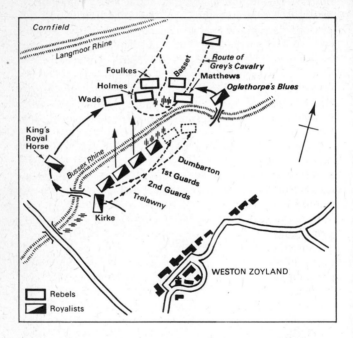

In February 1685 King Charles II died and his brother ascended the throne as James II. Although openly a Roman Catholic, James was sensible enough not to antagonize Parliament on the matter of his religion and took the Coronation Oath to 'uphold the Government both in Church and State as by law established'. He had many followers who sympathized with his religious views and who might have supported him 'leading England back to Rome'. A split in the country on religious grounds was not impossible.

But all religious differences were set aside when the news came from Lyme Regis in June 1685. The Duke of Monmouth, an illegitimate son of Charles II, had landed with 300 men – and £80 in cash – to claim the throne. He declared he had been born in wedlock, was the rightful King of England and that his uncle, James II, was the usurper. Monmouth was joined by 3,000 men, mostly local militia or ignorant peasantry, many armed with only pitchforks and scythes though ready for an adventure. Barely half of them had firearms.

In the next three weeks Monmouth had himself proclaimed King in the market place at Taunton and gathered another 4,000 men – who cannot be called soldiers. However, trying to capture Bristol he was badly repulsed. The morale of his now considerable force was shaken and he withdrew to Taunton. A rebellion on the defensive is lost.

Part of the royal army was now collecting round Bath under Feversham, while John Churchill, later Duke of Marlborough, was concentrating other forces near Salisbury. Monmouth, hearing of the friction between Feversham and Churchill, moved forward again to Bridgewater, while the royal forces, now united, marched down from Bath, bivouacking in and around the village of Weston Zoyland, 3 miles to the east of Bridgewater, on the night of 15 June. Next day the last battle on English soil was to be fought. Several English regiments were to fight their first engagement.

During the evening of the 15th incorrect reports reached Monmouth that there was much drunkenness and disorder in the royal camp and that its vigilance and preparedness were poor.

Accordingly he decided upon the desperate adventure of a night advance across the damp, boggy Sedgemoor and an attack at dawn on, he hoped, the comatose royal troops asleep in their bivouacs. A similar mad venture was to be tried by another rebel royal prince 61 years later, when Bonnie Prince Charlie marched by night from Culloden across its moor to Nairn, there hoping, but failing, to surprise Cumberland's army.

Prima facie, Monmouth's plan was good. He outnumbered Feversham's army by at least two to one and he knew the English people and their army were lukewarm towards James. Considerable desertions might be expected, while a quick success at dawn might cause the royal troops to withdraw or declare for him. Had Feversham's army been dispersed, Monmouth must have seized the crown and a Protestant Stuart dynasty must have been firmly established yet again. Once more the future monarchy of England was to be decided by a brief battle. Bosworth and Naseby were to be repeated.

Monmouth's night march was a nightmare. The darkness, the loss of direction due to the necessity of avoiding a Royalist cavalry outpost at Chedzoy, the delay in finding a crossing of a large ditch, the Langmoor Rhine, the confusion when the rebel columns found themselves barred by another ditch, the Bussex Rhine, all combined to throw the untrained near-civilian army of Monmouth into great disarray. At about 2 am, while waiting for the crossing of the Langmoor Rhine to be found, the rebels waiting impatiently sat down and, despite orders to the contrary, started to chat. The talking inevitably spread and a trooper of the Blues out in the night scouting heard the buzz of conversation. Firing his pistol as a warning he galloped back to Feversham's army at Weston Zoyland, calling out: 'Beat the drums, the enemy is here, stand to.' At once the Royalist soldiers fell in at their alarm posts.

The six regiments moved out of Weston Zoyland and took up a position half a mile to the north-west of the village, overlooking the Bussex Rhine and 200 yards short of it. Covering a frontage of about half a mile, two battalions of Dumbarton's

Regiment (now the Royal Scots) were on the right of the line, on their left being the Grenadier Guards and the Coldstream, then the King's Own and on the extreme left flank the Queen's Regiment.

About 2 am the rebels, having crossed the Langmoor Rhine, were approaching the Bussex Rhine. Lord Grey, in charge of the rebel horse, galloped forward with his men to reconnoitre the Bussex Rhine and to find a crossing. He had been told that two existed, about three-quarters of a mile apart. But his men were not very effective. Riding up and down the Rhine looking for the two crossings they were seen from the far side by the royal regiments in the gathering light. Received with volleys of musketry they panicked and rode off the field, causing great confusion to their own infantrymen coming up behind them.

These were now approaching the Bussex Rhine and as they came up to the ditch were in full view of the Guards, the King's Own and the Queen's. Instead of crossing the Rhine, which was found to be almost dry, they halted and began a fire-fight across the ditch. Although barely half were armed with muskets they took on the solid phalanxes of six regular infantry battalions. These infantry regiments, although their loyalty for James may have been doubtful, were incensed at the presumption of a 'foreign' force landing on English soil. Monarchy and religion were of secondary importance. At Sedgemoor the men were concerned only with throwing this interloper off their native soil. Their musketry was excellent.

Monmouth tried to persuade his rabble to advance too and cross the ditch. But the rebels, realizing what was in front of them, refused to budge.

Owing to the slightly devious path Monmouth had taken through the night to avoid the cavalry outpost at Chedzoy the weight of his advance had come against the right-hand battalions, the Royal Scots. Three brass guns of the rebels were brought forward to within 160 yards to play on the regiment, and it suffered severely, all but four of its officers becoming casualties. John Churchill, seeing this pressure on his right flank, and that the Queen's and the King's Own on the left had not been heavily engaged so far, brought these two regiments round behind the Guards and the Royal Scots to prolong the line to the right. The King's Own were now on the extreme right and in the most exposed position should the rebels find a crossing in a flank attack.

But the fire-effect of the royal line was increasing and the rebels, already unsteady, began to disintegrate. By 5 am many individuals were leaving the field and by full daylight the battle was over. All Monmouth's men were running.

The exact positions occupied by the English regiments cannot be accurately determined today. The Bussex Rhine was filled in many years ago and only one or two very minor indentations in the fields indicate where it may have run. In Weston Zoyland Church is a modern photostat copy of a map made by the vicar on the day of the battle. It is vague but, although showing the Bussex Rhine clearly, indicates no other physical features. It is impossible to pinpoint it.

Towards the centre of the line and about 500 yards back from the Rhine is the battle memorial. It stands on the north side of the Langmoor Drove, a wide, unmetalled and in wet weather impassable cart-track.

The memorial, a granite post about 5 feet high, is enclosed by four small 'staddle-stones', bearing these names:

1700	1800
Plassey	Trafalgar
Quebec	Waterloo

1600	1900
Sedgemoor	The Great War
	1914–1918

The selection of these six names is curious, especially that of Trafalgar.

Five royal soldiers were buried in Weston Zoyland Church and 14 in the churchyard, but the position of the graves is uncertain and the names are unknown. It is probable that these 19 died in the village or in the church from wounds received on the battlefield, while those killed in the action itself were buried where they fell.

In the museum in Bridgewater is a 'Sedgemoor Room' with a good number of relics from the battle. An excellent panorama of the battle is shown with many metal toy soldiers. The six royal battalions, with their colours, are in position short of the Bussex Rhine, the King's Own and the Queen's being shown in their first positions before their move to the right flank.

The whole area of the battlefield, although much drained today, is still very wet and too damp for sheep grazing. Gum-boots are essential and the many wide field-drains, which are full of water, make movement very restricted. In the winter the moor and its droves must be almost impassable but it is well worth a visit in the summer.

Killiecrankie (1689)

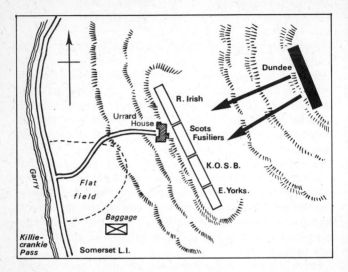

In June 1688 several members of Parliament in London, both Whigs and Tories, invited Prince William of Orange, a grandson of Charles I, and his wife Mary, daughter of James II, to come over to England as joint monarchs. James had so exasperated the English people by his blatant favouritism of Roman Catholics and his attempts to force that religion on the country that they felt only such a drastic step was of any use. In November 1688 William landed at Torbay.

A month after William and Mary were crowned at Westminster in April 1689 a deputation from Scotland offered them the Scottish crown. Both took the Coronation Oath that they would govern Scotland according to its laws, and William thus became the last King of Scotland, before the union of the crowns in 1707.

Although Scotland had declared for William it was really only the Lowlands that supported him. The Highlands were turbulent and uncertain, the old clan spirit being very much alive and the most powerful political factor in Scotland.

A month after William's coronation John Graham of Claverhouse, 'Bonny Dundee', disappeared from Edinburgh. He moved north into the Gordon country towards Inverness, recruiting over 1,000 followers. This event greatly alarmed the authorities in Edinburgh. They had only very recently accepted William as their sovereign and they believed that any revolt against, or even opposition to, the English government now would be not only breaking their covenant but very unwise politically.

Accordingly they despatched General Mackay, the commander of the forces in Scotland, with the Scottish Brigade, recently returned from Holland, to march north to 'find' Dundee.

Mackay set out from Edinburgh in the middle of April with 400 men and two troops of horse to carry out his mission, but reached Elgin and Inverness without finding his quarry, who had moved south almost to Perth. Mackay then realized that a much bigger force was needed to comb the Highlands efficiently and he withdrew, reaching Edinburgh on 1 July, leaving Dundee somewhere in the central Highlands round Blair Athol, neither defeated nor subdued. He marched out of Perth on the 26th in his second attempt to find and deal with Dundee.

He had some 4,500 regulars under his command, the Somerset Light Infantry, the East Yorks, the 18th Royal Irish, the Scots Fusiliers and the very newly raised King's Own Scottish Borderers. None of these units had very much experience and the oldest, the Somerset Light Infantry, had existed for only two years. The first night's halt was at Dunkeld, where at midnight Mackay heard from Lord

Murray, whom he had sent forward to secure Athole Castle
– now Blair Athol – that Dundee had come south again, was
in occupation of the whole of the Athole district and was in
the castle. Murray's message added that owing to his small
numbers he had retreated down the narrow and difficult pass
of Killiecrankie.

Early next morning Mackay marched on towards the pass,
which he reached at 11 am. He entered it with his whole force,
except the Somerset Light Infantry, which he left behind to
guard the baggage and to act as a rear-guard.

The pass is almost 3 miles long and runs through a mass of
steep, almost sheer, precipices. A handful of men on these
heights provided with stones and boulders could cause great
delay to the progress of an army.

Dundee, hearing that Mackay had entered the pass in
strength, decided that he must take a hand himself. Accordingly he marched out of Athole Castle and after 5 miles
turned off to the left at Glen Tilt until he gained high ground
near Urrard House. His army consisted of the Clan Maclean,
who held his right flank, while on the left he stationed some
not fully organized Macdonalds. In the centre he had the four
clan-regiments of Cameron, Macdonell, Clanranald and an
Irish regiment, all of which were semi-trained, possessing
some discipline and cohesion.

By 4 pm Mackay had cleared the pass with the greater part
of his force and had formed them up on a flat low field alongside the river, near today's village of Aldclune. On Mackay's
arrival on the flat ground beyond the pass he could see
Dundee's position now being occupied above Urrard House
on the right flank. Between the low ground and Dundee's
position stands a low eminence some 70 feet high and about
600 yards long, then as now covered with trees and shrubs.
It was within musket range of Mackay's force, now lying
down, and it was evident that it must be occupied before

Dundee moved forward, and downhill, in his attack, which seemed imminent. Accordingly Mackay ordered every regiment to stand up, make a right wheel, and advance up the ridge. He there took up a position facing Dundee's hill. All units formed up in half-battalion formation, with one half some distance behind the half in front. On the extreme left were the Royal Irish, then the Scots Fusiliers, the King's Own Scottish Battalion and on the right the East Yorks.

The Somerset Light Infantry had now emerged from the pass and the battalion took up a position behind the right forward battalion, the East Yorks. Its task was to prevent Dundee turning Mackay's right flank and so coming between it and the entrance to the pass.

The afternoon was now passing, and Mackay became fearful of a night attack and still more of a night retreat. Consequently, he tried various expedients to provoke the enemy to fight. Sorties from the second line went out, fully intending to return when they had 'drawn' the enemy. But all to no avail. Dundee was determined not to be forced to attack until near sunset.

About 7 pm, with about an hour of daylight left, the Highlanders led by Dundee moved forward. The men were naked to their waists, an old custom among the warring clans, who believed in having no encumberances in battle beyond their muskets, which they did not think very much of anyway, and their broadswords. They advanced down their hill, quickening their pace, uttering a yell, a sight and sound calculated to shake Mackay's army. However the English stood firm and being elementarily disciplined held their fire until the Scotsmen were only a few yards away. Then a volley rang out which told with terrible effect on the thick and mostly disorganized masses advancing towards them. For a few moments only the advantage was at least six to one on the side of Mackay's men.

But their muskets were now fired and it look several minutes in those days for them to be reloaded. Bayonets which screwed into the muzzles clearly could not be fixed until after the discharge of the weapon and by the time the defenders were almost ready to receive the attackers the enemy were upon them. This time-lag between the most effective fire of the muskets and the fixing of the bayonet left the English regiments virtually defenceless for a few moments, a lapse of time that was to lead to their decimation. In the following weeks General Mackay invented a bayonet fitted with a ring that clipped over the muzzle, leaving it free yet secured to the barrel lower down, an invention, though modified, that is still in use today.

The Scots trusted solely to their swords. The more robust among them carried the two-handed sword, a fearful weapon which by its weight and sweep alone could cut a swath through the ranks.

The momentary vulnerability of Mackay's men, the *élan* of the attack and the broadswords created panic among the English and the regiments were in chaos in a few minutes. They gave way and the line was broken as the general had feared. The centre and most of the right flank disintegrated and Dundee, seeing the gap, charged with his cavalry, endeavouring to meet the few English cavalry on the field and then capture the guns in the rear. But the English cavalry could not face this attack and fled, while Dundee, by an extraordinary circumstance undoubtedly due to misunderstood orders, found himself almost alone behind the original line. Looking round for support he was shot dead.

Mackay then ordered his two remaining troops of horse to advance round the outer flank of what was left of the English line and thence to take the Scottish line in flank. It was a hazardous task but reflects Mackay's tactical skill. These two troops of not more than 30 men each could not expect to do more than mildly embarrass the triumphant Scotsmen in their victory over the disintegrating English regiments, and they turned out not to be reliable. Mackay himself accompanied the left-hand troop but it and the other troop going round the right flank turned back. The general, galloping on and presuming his horsemen were following him, found himself alone behind his enemy's line about the same time that Dundee found himself in an exactly similar situation behind the English position.

The Highlanders came on and, seeing the baggage wagons, gave up pursuit and thoroughly enjoyed themselves. All Mackay's unwounded men got away in the dusk and he was able to collect large numbers of fugitives, herded together by the two remaining troops of cavalry.

No attempt was made to re-enter the pass and after crossing over the river Garry Mackay halted to see whether he was being pursued. Nothing was seen or heard by the little cavalry rear-guard and after a brief rest the defeated army set off across country in the night. Thirty-six hours later, after a nightmare march, the army reached Stirling, having marched southward through Aberfeldy and Crieff, passing close to Gleneagles.

The field where Mackay first halted his regiments is easily found alongside the main Perth–Inverness road. It is a few hundred yards beyond the northern exit from the Pass. In the middle is a rough-hewn stone, 5 feet high with no inscription but which local legend says marks the site where the halted baggage wagons were plundered by Dundee's men. It is so isolated in this great field that it obviously commemorates something.

The eminence on Mackay's right is higher, steeper and more imposing than one might expect. The main hill occupied by the Highlanders, overlooking the ridge, is bare and its declivity is sufficient to have assisted the charge greatly. The quite considerable downhill run must have given Dundee's men enormous momentum and it is no wonder that the many survivors from the first and only English musketry volley easily overran the defenders.

Urrard House, standing in a delightful garden and grounds, is on the plateau made by the ridge before it rejoins the main hill. Its owner, Mr Hill-Wood, courteously allowed the author to see the house, which was rebuilt a few years ago and stands on the foundations of the house of 1689.

The Boyne (1690)

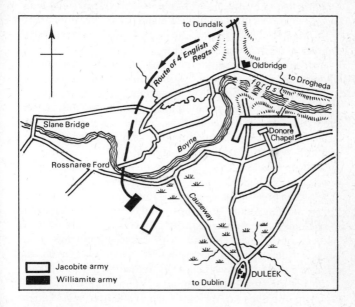

Succeeding his brother, Charles II, James II, although at heart a Roman Catholic, promised 'to uphold the Government both in Church and State as by law established'.

After a while he began to show favour to Roman Catholics. Protestant ministers were replaced and army officers had better chances of promotion if they 'belonged'. He then issued a Declaration of Indulgence suspending some penal laws against the Roman Catholics. This was too much for the leading Protestant members of Parliament and they quite illegally asked William Prince of Orange, grandson of Charles

I, to come over with his wife, Mary, daughter of the King, to rule England.

James fled to France on New Year's Day. There Louis XIV suggested that he should invade Ireland.

In March 1689 James landed at Kinsale with a large number of Irish, Scottish and English supporters, as well as French officers, arms and ammunition, and marched to Dublin where he was received with great rejoicings, the event being hailed as representing deliverance from English bondage.

This invasion of Ireland by James and his 3,000 Frenchmen had naturally caused London considerable concern. It became clear that a military expedition would be needed to re-establish William's authority in Ireland.

William was slightly doubtful of the English regular regiments. He had seen many of the men come over to him only a year previously, deserting James, and he did not care to risk sending many of them to Ireland, fearing that some might desert again. Consequently he brought 8,000 Dutch soldiers over from Holland with 2,500 Huguenots from France. Later these troops were stiffened by seven regular infantry battalions on whose loyalty William felt he could rely.

During the spring and summer of 1690 there was a steady build-up of troops for William's army in Ulster and William landed at Carrickfergus on 14 June. Two days later he marched out of Belfast towards Dundalk. James marched out of Dublin on the same day, also for Dundalk, and he reached the river Boyne.

In the centre of James's position on the south bank an acute curve in the Boyne creates a sharp northward-pointing salient. Opposite the tip of this salient was the hamlet of Oldbridge. Three miles farther upstream lay the next ford at Rossnaree, while half a mile downstream was another ford. Between these fords the river was impassable. James felt safe as he could see $1\frac{1}{2}$ miles away to his left a bog, which a local told him was impassable even to cavalry. Understandably he ignored the Rossnaree ford beyond the bog.

About a mile farther back from the Oldbridge ford ran an east–west ridge, on the top of which stood the village of Donore with its clearly seen church. Halfway down the north face of the ridge James posted his trained French troops, to act as a 'stop' in the event of the raw Irish troops in front giving way.

On 30 June William marched on to the high ground above the north bank of the Boyne. There on the opposite shore he could see the Jacobites' camp, where men were busy erecting breastworks along the river bank.

Under William were his own Dutch Guards, reputedly the best in Europe, English regiments, Scotsmen, Danes, Huguenots, Germans and stout-hearted Ulstermen. There was no lingua franca in William's army but there was discipline. He had 36,000 men, rather more than James.

The battle began early on 1 July with a large Williamite contingent consisting of the Queen's Regiment, the King's Own, the Somerset Light Infantry and the Welsh Fusiliers setting out in the darkness westward to capture the bridge at Slane 5 miles upstream from Oldbridge. The early dawn saw it a long way from its objective and in full view of James's army. It turned left, abandoning the plan to sieze the bridge and hoping to find a way across the river at the Rossnaree ford. It succeeded and crossed the river, but drew up on finding its way barred by the bog. Some cavalry from James's far right and the majority of the French regulars from in front of Donore moved out to meet this threat.

Meanwhile William made a major advance against the Oldbridge ford. The Dutch Guards led, advancing down the high ground on the north bank via a ravine still known as King William's Glen. Plunging into the river eight abreast, up to their chests in the water, they crossed the ford under heavy but not very accurate fire from the south bank. They succeeded in reaching the far side and establishing themselves among the defending Irish, where hand-to-hand mêlées took place. To advance through 60 yards of water 4 feet deep, against close musketry, and there repel constant cavalry charges was a military feat that has received insufficient recognition by historians.

These excellent Dutch soldiers were regulars of the best sort. They had little concern with politics or religion and did only as they were told. They had little interest in Ireland, or in England, except that their prince was now England's king.

The Dutch were closely followed through the river by the Huguenots. They were different from the Dutch soldiers. Not so well trained or disciplined, they possessed another quality – burning eagerness to take on the hated papists whose religion had so cruelly persecuted their parents at the time of the revocation of the Edict of Nantes. Forced to flee their country, mostly to Holland, they welcomed a chance to pay back old scores.

About midday William, supervising the operations at Oldbridge, heard that yet another ford existed a mile farther downstream. Leading his Inniskilling, Dutch and Danish cavalry in person he crossed without great opposition. Galloping on, he fetched a wide circle round the mêlée of Irish cavalry and Dutch and Huguenot infantry at the Oldbridge ford, and rode up into the village of Donore, $1\frac{1}{2}$ miles from Oldbridge.

Indescribable confusion reigned in the streets of Donore. In the rough and tumble a few men were inadvertently killed or wounded by their own friends, and William himself had a narrow escape. One soldier pointed his firearm at him but William, pushing it calmly aside, said, 'I am the king. Fire at the enemy'.

Meanwhile, on James's left flank, the British infantry felt

that they could get through the bog. Probing for a way they quickly found that the ground, although soft, was little more than very rough commonland, covered with waist-high grass. As though on a vast partridge drive the leading regiments, the King's Own and the Welsh Fusiliers, advanced holding their muskets above their shoulders, the two other infantry battalions closely following. It must have made a wonderful sight.

James, who had come down to reorganize his French troops to meet this threat, heard that the Irish had given way at Oldbridge and that Williams's cavalry were in Donore. Outflanked on his right by William's cavalry work, his left about to be enveloped by the passage of the bog and his centre collapsed by the evacuating Irish, he and his army had no alternative but flight.

William pursued James's cavalry for only 7 miles. He has been criticized for not 'improving' his victory and thereby preventing so many of the enemy getting away. But it is probable that he did not want to risk capturing James – and thereby saddling himself with an embarrassing prisoner. For the *de facto* King of England to have what many considered the *de jure* King of England under his guard, and in a semiforeign country, would have created untold complications.

It was not an overwhelming victory. William lost 500 men from all causes, while James left 1,500 men on the field, many of them prisoners, and all his few guns and his baggage train. The Danish Life Guards, who were in William's left-flank attack across the lower ford, is the only regiment in the world to bear the battle honour 'the Boyne' on its colours.

Donore is only a cluster of cottages today, with a modern church, at a crossroads. Half a mile to the south, and on a pronounced hill, lie the remains of the church standing in

King William III at the battle of the Boyne

1690. In the churchyard are several very old yew trees and they and the church must have been visible for many miles. The vista northwards from the churchyard is magnificent and the ford at Oldbridge, King William's Glen and the high ground beyond the Boyne are clearly visible. Oldbridge hamlet on the north bank has disappeared, but King William's Glen, still so called and marked on the map, is very clear. Running sharply uphill for a mile it could easily conceal many thousands of men, and as a covered approach to a battlefield could not be bettered. The ford has been replaced by a fine iron bridge, but its site is clear. It passed precisely under the line of the present bridge and on the south side the remains of the 'way' climbing the bank can still be seen.

The ground on which the Dutch Guards and the Huguenots fought the Irish infantry is now the park of the local big house and sloping gradually up from the river makes an excellent site for defensive tactics.

The ford at Rossnaree where the four English regiments crossed is shown by broken water in an otherwise placid, smoothly flowing sheet of water. The bog is very evident. Two hundred yards above the ford is a very old watermill, owned by an old Irish peasant and his sister. Both declare that the mill has been in the possession of their family for many hundreds of years and they are certain that their ancestor saw the troops crossing in 1690.

Siege of Limerick (1690)

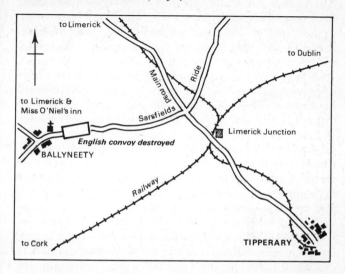

After William III's victory at the Battle of the Boyne on 1 July James II fled to France, never to leave it again. William led his army southward, dispersing isolated pockets of Irish patriots and French soldiers left behind by James, and by 9 August reached Limerick. Finding its gates closed against him he summoned it to surrender. The governor, a Frenchman, replied 'that he was too honoured at being besieged by so great a prince as not to make every effort to resist'.

Trenches were dug, guns brought up, others were sent for from Cashel and on 10 August the siege began. A complete line of trenches did not encircle the town leaving no exit; rather several detached and separate forces stood to at dawn each day on a vast perimeter with many uncovered gaps. The

Irish army was mostly within the walled area. Some were on
King's Island within the great loop the Shannon makes round
the town, others in Irishtown where the main gate to the
fortress lay. One large force of Irish cavalry, under a Colonel
Sarsfield, was lying near the present Ardnacrusha power
station, 2 miles out to the north.

On 12 August word reached the city that William's
additional guns required for the siege had left Cashel escorted
by the Bays. Sarsfield was sent for and ordered to intercept
them and he left at 9 pm on an historic cavalry foray. Covering
35 miles before giving his men and horses water and a brief
rest, he covered another 25 miles and reached a little village,
Cullen, near Tipperary. Here, a story runs, they met an old
woman bathing her feet in a stream. She was taken into an
inn and plied with whisky and beer. Eventually she disclosed
that the guns were 5 miles up the road at the next village,
Ballyneety, halted for the night. She added that the password
was 'Sarsfield'. This improbable story is very much a local
legend in the Ballyneety district and is given in full in
brochures issued by the Limerick town council and the
Shannonside tourism organization. But it does not stand up
to examination. The stream where the old lady was said to be
bathing her feet is $3\frac{1}{2}$ miles from Ballyneety and it is extremely
unlikely that she would have walked so far. It is impossible
to believe that a soldier of the cavalry escort to the guns would
have betrayed the password to a passing woman in an
obviously unfriendly district. But if she had overheard
'careless talk' among the Bays from behind a hedge, it would
mean little to her, and the soldiers' English accent would be
difficult for her to understand. Lastly, surely it is too much
of a coincidence that the escort commander would choose the
word 'Sarsfield' on the very night Sarsfield was to attack him.

Sarsfield's men moved off at dawn and found the guns set
up in full readiness along the road. The only sentry did not

see them and the sleeping guard was killed to a man. The main body of the escort, the Bays, woke up, and all the men were killed or captured. The eight guns were filled with powder, their muzzles buried in the soft ground; a train was laid, everyone moved to safety and the fuse was lit. A tremendous explosion destroyed the guns, wagons, ammunition and supplies, but Sarsfield's party did not get off without opposition. A small party of English cavalry, the 6th Inniskilling Dragoons, were sent out from Limerick to meet the guns and, coming down the road, heard the noise and charged. A few of Sarsfield's men were killed but the vast majority got away, with the draught-horses from the guns and the mounts of the escort. Returning by an even more circuitous route than the outward journey they eventually reached Limerick after a total ride of 160 miles in six days.

The loss of the guns was a severe strategic blow to William and a psychological one to his men in the trenches. A half-hearted attack led by the Norfolks on an existing narrow breach in the walls was easily repulsed, with some loss, and on the following day it started to rain. The trenches were soon flooded, fever appeared, the English soldiers were utterly miserable and a few days later William raised the siege. He marched his men away from the city to such winter quarters as the hostile Irish peasantry in villages and small towns could be forced to offer. The men had spent three of the worst weeks, climate-wise, the British army had ever spent, not incomparable to Passchendaele in October 1917.

Large sections of the walls can be seen where St Peter's Street crosses Bishop's Street, behind West Watergate, and by St John's Hospital, where the massive gateways were one of the entrances through the walls.

Most of these surviving bits of wall are about 15 feet high, but none is longer than 30 yards. The gap in the centre of the West Watergate relic-wall was one of the lesser gateways of the city and local legend says that through it Sarsfield went on his historic ride.

Apart from the very considerable remains of the walls, there are a number of very old masonry blocks, mostly built on to by more modern houses. They are very apparent and seem to have been part of substantial buildings within the walls, possibly barracks, or houses of important people. It is difficult to decide whether these odd pieces of masonry are bolstered up by the more modern buildings or vice versa.

King John's Castle, in Castle Street, immediately to the east of Thomond bridge, was built in 1210 and shows several patches of brickwork, the repairs to holes made by English guns in 1690.

A visit to Ballyneety (on the road from Pallas Green to Emly 20 miles south-east from Limerick) is worth while. The actual site of the night attack on the guns can be precisely fixed. The road here is a sunken one running between banks 5 feet high, with hedges today, and probably in 1690, along their tops. To have halted a convoy of precious guns in this defile for the night could hardly have been more culpable. Infantry could approach unseen in the dark to within 5 yards, and the mounted escort could operate in defence only by climbing the bank on foot. Had the guard been awake the noise of Sarsfield's cavalry must have alerted them sufficiently to stand to the whole escort. The tactical knowledge and control over his doubtless tired men by this officer of the Bays, Captain Pulteney, left much to be desired.

Some miles nearer to Limerick at a crossroads stands a whitewashed pub, where tradition says the Inniskilling Dragoons stopped for a drink on the way down to Ballyneety to meet the guns. It is virtually unaltered since 1690 and the owner, Miss O'Neil, is not only very proud of her building but also extremely knowledgeable about the history both of this campaign and of her district.

Siege of Cork (1690)

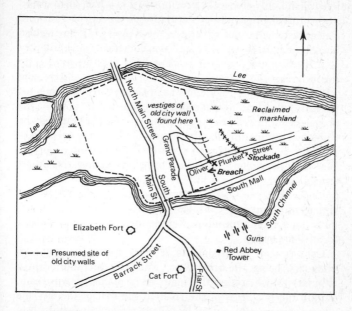

After William's withdrawal from Limerick and his army's occupation of winter quarters the morale of the still un-defeated Irish rose considerably. The French on the continent were still very aggressive and their naval victory off Beachy Head caused William, now back in London, grave concern. He feared another French landing in southern Ireland and knew that immediate and enthusiastic support by the Irish for the French was inevitable. To prevent the French using two Southern Irish ports, Cork and Kinsale, an expedition of five regiments, the King's Own, Royal Fusiliers, King's and Somerset Light Infantry, landed at Cork Harbour to prevent any French troops landing nearby. Two of these four regiments, the King's Own and the Somerset Light Infantry, had left Ireland only six weeks previously. They had participated in the great flank march at the Battle of the Boyne and were well accustomed to active service, the King's Own having also been at Sedgemoor in 1685, and the Somerset Light Infantry at Killiecrankie in 1689. It has not been possible to identify the fifth regiment. Usually an infallible method of discovering whether a particular regiment was present at an engagement is to study the battle honours on the colours, but none of the engagements in the Irish campaigns of 1690 appears on the colours of any regiments, the enemy having been subjects of the king. For this reason none of the battles of the American War of Independence nor the campaigns against the Stuart risings of 1715 and 1745 appear today on any colours.

Under Marlborough's command the five regiments disembarked 7 miles up Cork Harbour, near Blackrock. Stores, guns, food and ammunition were landed, and two days later an advance began.

Cork lay on an island, as it does today, its northern boundary being the river Lee, while on the south ran a tributary which joined the main river a mile downstream. Within the two arms of the river to the east of the city the ground was marshy, cut up by several streams and difficult to cross. Just outside the city wall the defenders had built a stockade about where Grand Parade runs today.

Over the southern tributary lay two forts, Elizabeth Fort, opposite the south-west corner of the walls where Barrack Street now runs, and Cat Fort, overlooking Friar Street.

Marlborough marched up the right bank of the southern tributary and captured Cat Fort, leaving Elizabeth Fort alone. Siege guns were brought up to near Cat Fort and a bombardment opened to make a breach in the walls at their south-east corner. At the same time 5,000 Danish and Dutch troops marched up the north bank to seal off the northern exits from the city. Three days later the guns had made a breach and an assault was possible.

The Irish governor of Cork, feeling that discretion was best, sent out an envoy to seek terms. He went to the Duke of Württemberg's camp first, but was told that it was Marlborough's turn to command that day (a not uncommon practice for commanders of great seniority or royal rank in those days), and that he must apply to Marlborough. The delay caused by going to the wrong headquarters prevented negotiations for a settlement which might have been successful. By now the high tide covered the marshy ground in front of the breach. Next morning, however, the bombardment recommenced and, the tide being out, 1,000 Danes crossed the northern arm of the Lee while 1,500 men, mostly grenadiers, of the King's Own, Royal Fusiliers and Somerset Light Infantry moved down to the bank of the southern tributary and waded across to the marsh, holding their arms and ammunition above their heads to keep them dry. They were met by fire from the stockade but, not pausing, drove these outposts back to the breach, and through the walls. Here the troops reformed for an assault, but the white flag went up and the four regiments entered the town. Four thousand Irish soldiers were captured for an unknown but minute number of English casualties.

The city of Cork now has a population of 120,000 (1971). Buildings of all sorts have now overflowed across both arms of the river and the walls have virtually disappeared. It is probable, no more, that the eastern wall ran along Grand Parade. Down Oliver Plunket Street and 40 yards beyond its junction with Grand Parade on the right lies Conway's Yard, where a small repair garage is situated. At its far end, and in the left-hand corner, is a considerable mass of probably

seventeenth-century masonry. It must have been out slightly
beyond the general line of the wall and is possibly the remains
of one of the bastions.

Elizabeth and Cat Forts are easily found in Barrack Street
and Friar Street respectively. Cat Fort has only one of its
gigantic outer walls left and is not very interesting but
Elizabeth Fort has much to show. It has its four outer walls,
forming a quadrilateral, quite unchanged and in wonderful
condition. It is now used as a police barracks and the married
quarters face on to the great inner courtyard. Surprisingly
there is no trace of a moat.

Main gate into Elizabeth Fort

The contrast between the austere, massive and forbidding walls of the two forts and the mean Victorian narrow streets all round them is most striking. Their tactical position, on high ground overlooking the lower arm of the river Lee and then the city-on-the-island as it was is, *per se*, excellent.

These forts left the three other sides of the walled town unguarded, although on the north side of the town lies more high ground, also suitable for forts.

Siege of Kinsale (1690)

Immediately after the capitulation of Cork, Marlborough marched his five regiments down to Kinsale 17 miles away. The harbour was as big as that of Cork, and in 1690 its facilities for anchorage and unloading were superior.

The town lies on the northern shore of the river Bandon, protected on its landward side in 1690 by considerable fortifications, following a perimeter of about a mile. Below the town lay two forts, Old Fort on the southern bank, opposite the town on a tongue of land made by a big loop of the river, while Fort Charles faced Old Fort across the water.

Kinsale was reached by Marlborough's army after a two-day march virtually across country, the roads being barely worth the name, in time to seize the town and prevent the Irish setting fire to it. The troops were billeted in the town and greatly appreciated the shelter from the atrocious weather.

Two days after their arrival 800 Danes were ferried across the Bandon in the night and landing below Old Fort carried it by storm from the rear. The Fort's outlook, both material and psychological, was seaward, and like Singapore in 1941 it had neglected the landward approach from the rear.

But Fort Charles, across the water, was a very different proposition. Its landward, northern, face was well fortified and strongly held and it was believed that the loss of Old Fort would concentrate all resistance, both military and patriotic, in this last position of Irish cohesion. (See plan, p. 258.)

Clearly the assault must await the siege-train of guns, which had already been much delayed by the weather and absence of roads on its journey from Cork. The English army marched out from the town, surrounded the fort and dug trenches only 200 yards out from the escarpment.

Battery positions were constructed for the guns and the army settled down in great discomfort to starve the garrison out. However, the guns arrived five days later and were at once mounted in the positions awaiting them. Fire was opened with excellent results and four days later a general assault was about to begin.

The Irish however asked for terms, and with his men already suffering severely from the appalling weather, Marlborough allowed the garrison generous conditions, one being permission to march away to Limerick with all their arms and baggage.

The English regiments were in poor shape. The incessant rain, mud, humidity and lack of shelter at night had greatly lowered their health and in the month's campaign over 400 men had died from disease, with many more in hospital. The King's Own alone had 220 men off duty at the capitulation of Kinsale.

There is no record of casualties sustained in the 1690 campaign but the few that did occur were far outweighed by disease. It is probable that the conditions suffered by the troops in this very wet autumn coupled with the understandable hostility of the Irish peasants were as bad as any suffered before the First World War.

A visit to Kinsale must centre round Fort Charles. This gigantic fortress, rebuilt in 1670 on the foundations of its predecessor of 1500, is a striking ruin in remarkable condition. It covers several acres, its outer 'curtain' and bastions and the moat being 80 per cent as they were in 1690. Few of the buildings within the perimeter are less than 20 feet high, while all are standing up to the first storey.

Tactically its position is superb. It entirely covers the comparatively narrow entrance to the magnificent Kinsale harbour, and its guns could pursue ships that had slipped past below the fortress and were turning into Kinsale's inner harbour. Tactically it is very similar to Fort Staddon, overlooking Plymouth Sound.

Marlborough's batteries were on the highish ground to the south-east. They largely dominated the fort, but they were outgunned by the heavier and better protected Irish pieces. It is surprising that the Irish capitulated without a fight, when they held the cards of superior weapons, shelter from the weather, cover from fire, their backs to the water, and patriotism.

Old Fort, on its promontory sticking out into the river, has almost disappeared. The few pieces of masonry on its 'coll' – surrounded by a number of turf-covered mounds – are rather disappointing. The little masonry surviving, when compared with Fort Charles, indicates clearly that its position, tactically too good to be true, attracted and suffered much from concentrated bombardment from hostile ships.

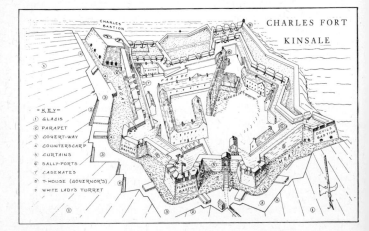

CHARLES FORT
KINSALE

- K E Y -
① GLACIS
② PARAPET
③ COVERT-WAY
④ COUNTERSCARP
⑤ CURTAINS
⑥ SALLY-PORTS
⑦ CASEMATES
⑧ T-HOUSE (GOVERNOR'S)
⑨ WHITE LADY'S TURRET

There are isolated traces of the town walls (mostly demolished before 1690) near Rose Abbey, Market Street, Main Street and Mill Hill.

Old-world Kinsale Town, its forts, walls and harbour belong to the eighteenth century – except in July and August.

Glencoe (1692)

In 1688 several members of the English Parliament, exasperated at James II's religious bigotry and dictatorship, invited William of Orange, grandson of Charles I, and Mary, his wife, daughter of James II, to come over to rule England. James ran away to France, and William and Mary ascended the throne of England. By James's desertion of his post the throne of Scotland also became vacant and Scotland duplicated England's invitation to William.

William was acclaimed King of Scotland in London; he was the last King of Scotland. At once he adopted Presbyterianism as the state religion and immediately set the Highlands, its clans and its episcopacy in a blaze. The clans' Scottish nationality dwindled but their clannishness emerged in increasing strength. It became a silent protest against their government in Edinburgh accepting a foreign Protestant monarch. The fact that William III was the grandson of Charles I – a Stuart – and was therefore quarter Stuart himself made little difference.

The Highlanders, mostly Episcopalians, and the Lowlanders, the Presbyterians, had constant wrangles. William regarded these petty squabbles in Scotland as just an annoyance and he determined to put a stop to them so that he could concentrate on more important issues.

As a start £12,000 was distributed among the clan chiefs as a bribe to be loyal to William. But some of the chiefs refused to be bought off, while others pocketed their share but did not alter their ways. The next step was to lead to the massacre of Glencoe.

The Marquess of Breadalbane, a leading Scottish politician, had engineered the distribution of the £12,000. He was a

Campbell with a built-in dislike of any Macdonald. The Campbells, in the course of the feud against the Macdonalds, had been guilty of far more raids, thefts and cruelties than the Macdonalds. They were deservedly regarded by them with hatred. Although never likely to turn the other cheek, the Macdonalds' record would bear comparison with that of the Campbells. They did, however, indulge in the occasional raid on Campbell cattle.

The Secretary of State, Sir John Dalrymple and the Master of Stair, also a Campbell, a most able man and a trained lawyer with the precise lawyer's disapproval of lawless people – or clans – together with Breadalbane issued the famous ultimatum of August 1691. It required all chieftains to take an oath of allegiance to the king by 1 January 1692, threatening that failure to comply would be 'punished by fire and sword'.

In the intervening four months the large majority of the chieftains had taken the oath, one of the exceptions being Macdonald of Glencoe.

Hamilton, governor of Fort William, was to inform Stair whether he thought January with its heavy snow was a good time to maul the Macdonalds, and that if so he was to be ready by 1 January.

On 15 December several regular Scottish regiments marched out of Perth and Stirling north-westward, to Fort William, north of Glencoe. In Inveraray, to the south, 800 men of the Earl of Argyll's Regiment were stationed. The Macdonalds in Glencoe were surrounded by menacing forces, known to be unfriendly, yet with no *casus belli*.

Late at night on 30 December Alasdair Macdonald, chief of the Macdonalds of Glencoe, the only chief who had not yet subscribed to the oath of allegiance, arrived at the Castle of Inverlochy to take the oath. Macdonald was told that he must go to the sheriff, a Campbell, at Inveraray, nearly 50 miles

away. The old man and his retinue of six gillies had a nightmare march of two days and three nights to reach Inveraray at
dawn on 2 January. With some ceremony the oath was
administered and taken in semi-public. Macdonald, much
relieved at his success, returned to Glencoe, where he called
his clan together at his house, Carnoch, telling them that he
had taken an oath in their name as well as in his own as
chieftain, and ordered them to obey King William III and his
government. All were now within the law and nothing more
was to be feared. The Macdonalds heaved a sigh of relief and
that night slept peacefully in their beds. The commander of
the garrison at Fort William wrote to Macdonald soon after,
telling him that he and his people were now under the
protection of the military.

But the Macdonalds were living in a fool's paradise. On
about 10 January, Stair, then in London, heard that Macdonald had in fact taken the oath, although outside the time-
limit. Saying that he was sorry that Glencoe was safe, he
ordered Hamilton, governor of Fort William, to order two
companies of the Earl of Argyll's Regiment under Captain
Campbell of Glenlyon to march for Glencoe.

Glenlyon was 60 years of age, a gambler, a heavy drinker,
brave, of florid good looks. As a younger man women had
considered him an Adonis and his manners were still polished
and charming. With men he was robustly jovial, using
Christian names freely, was acceptable, popular and trusted,
but treacherous.

His two companies arrived at Ballachulish on 1 February,
where they were seen and reported to Macdonald at his house
4 miles away. Macdonald sent his son John, whose judgement
he could trust, to meet the soldiers and to make them welcome
if they came in peace.

'We come as friends', Lieutenant Lindsay, the subaltern,
replied, and then stood aside and Glenlyon came forward with

outstretched hand. Greeting young Macdonald boisterously he asked for news of the family, and then inquired about what quarters could be made available in the bad weather. John replied that the soldiers were welcome in Glencoe and walked back alongside Glenlyon at the head of his troops to the chieftain's house. Here the old man met the party, with his wife at his side, and repeated his son's assurance of a welcome. Glenlyon's officers were then introduced, each removing his hat and bowing.

The soldiers were quartered four or five to a cottage from Carnoch eastward, covering a distance along the glen of about 3 miles. Glenlyon, refusing the chief's offer of hospitality, was billeted with another Macdonald at Inverrigan, about a mile from Carnoch. There were altogether six officers and 130 men in the party.

The soldiers spent the mornings drilling, the villagers watching with amusement for a few days. Some of them however complained to Macdonald about the presence of the soldiers, but were told that hospitality had been offered and accepted and gradually the soldiers were taken to the hearts of their hosts. In the afternoons the Campbells and the Macdonalds joined in the games of wrestling, throwing the stone and tossing the caber. Archery, sword-dancing and bagpipe competitions were held and much whisky was consumed in the evenings round the peat fires. Glenlyon, drinking heavily, gambled with his host Inverrigan, and with Alasdair Macdonald's sons. Frequently he dined at Carnoch. The atmosphere in the glen between the Campbells and the Macdonalds could hardly have been more amicable. The Macdonalds, who had for generations hated the Campbells, began to wonder whether they were, in fact, not at all bad. Hospitality and its acceptance increased. Rarely can a body of people have been so lured into a sense of false security, so duped, so betrayed.

On 12 February 400 men from Fort William marched down to Ballachulish to block the western exit from Glencoe while another 400 marched over the mountains to the south-east and descended into the glen to stop up the eastern exit. On the same day Hamilton sent a written order from Fort William to Glenlyon in Glencoe to put to the sword all Macdonald men under 70. In particular the chief and his sons were to be killed. All exits from the glen were to be secured, and the killing was to start at 5 am.

This order was handed to Glenlyon as he was playing cards with Alasdair Macdonald's sons at Inverrigan. He at once decided to act. Sending for his officers, he told each to call their men together out of doors where no voices could be heard and to warn them for an early parade under arms at 5 am next day.

By now many of the Campbell soldiers had become very fond of their hosts and suspecting that evil deeds would be perpetrated next morning advised several Macdonalds to spend the night away from the glen, despite the weather. John Macdonald saw many Campbell soldiers about late at night, far more than there had been in the past 12 days. Going to the chief he told him what he had seen, but the old man told him not to be foolish and that all was well.

Before dawn John was wakened by shouting in the night, and went to Glenlyon's headquarters at Inverrigan. There he saw the Campbell, and his officers and sergeants, loading their muskets.

The first man to be killed was Duncan Rankin, a servant at Carnoch, who, hearing a noise and seeing soldiers, ran off to the river and was shot as he fled. Lieutenant Lindsay then marched his men up to the Macdonald's house, and called out in a friendly voice for admittance. A servant woke the old man, saying that the Campbell soldiers had orders to march on, and wished to say '*au revoir*'. Macdonald got up, telling his wife to dress too, and said that they must speed the Campbells on their way with a glass of wine. Standing with his back to the door and pulling on his trews he heard the soldiers running up the stairs. Bursting into the bedroom Lindsay shot Macdonald twice and dragged his wife downstairs. There the soldiers drew her rings from her fingers and, tearing off her clothes, threw her out into the cold. She survived for three days.

This particular deed, the killing of the old man, in the presence of his wife, when only half-dressed, when getting up to entertain them with wine, was the one that shocked the world at the time and has done so ever since.

A mile farther up the glen at his house John Macdonald saw 20 soldiers slowly approaching through the snow. Miraculously he got his wife, children and servants out of the house and up to the cover of some trees on Meall Mor. The younger brother, Alasdair Og, made a similar escape, joining his family with his brother's in the trees. Here they all spent the remainder of the night – daylight did not come until nearly 9 am – and they could see the flames of Carnoch and Invercoe – another large house – in the darkness.

At Inverrigan, Glenlyon's headquarters, eight men were killed by the soldiers. These eight were Inverrigan's servants, who had been shackled in the cellars of the house during the night for some hours and were eventually shot outside on a dunghill, Glenlyon personally shooting his host. In nearby houses men were bayoneted in their beds.

At Achnacone, $1\frac{1}{2}$ miles farther up the glen, the worst carnage took place. Fourteen people were burned to death in one cottage, and an old man of 80 was murdered. Those few who escaped got through the snow and the darkness better than the soldiers, but some died of exposure on the hills.

The massacre of Glencoe was over and by the late afternoon the soldiers were gone. There was a smell of fire, blood and death everywhere in each hamlet. There were no voices or the lowing of cattle. The soldiers had taken 1,100 cows and horses, numberless sheep and goats. Clothing, jewels, kitchen utensils, silver cups, whisky, smoked fish, blankets from the beds, shoes, all were plundered. No fewer than 38 men had been killed and never was there stronger proof that the greatest tragedy of mankind is man's inhumanity to man.

Both sons of the old chief survived, and the elder, John, lived to the age of 83 to see his grandson command a regiment of Macdonalds at Prestonpans, 53 years later.

Today by far the greater part of the 6-mile-long glen is deserted. The hamlets of Achnacone and Inverrigan have utterly disappeared and there are no more than four or five isolated homesteads to be seen in this bleak, desolate yet supremely impressive 6 miles. Despite ample grazing space on the hillsides and along the road there are few sheep and fewer cattle to be seen. There are few birds, no horses and indeed little life of any sort. Even if the events of 1692 were not known, an atmosphere of subdued gloom would be inescapable. The National Trust of Scotland information bureau at Achnacone makes a break in the otherwise bleak, almost deserted glen. Within the spacious so-called fields, better described as enclosures, stand numberless isolated great stones, doubtless left from the Ice Age. Today they suggest gravestones. Around them the few birds glide, but they do not sing.

But at the far end, the western end, of the glen, life is found again. A crossroads, with two garages and a hotel, leads to the village, today known as Glencoe but in the days of the massacre as Carnoch. Nearly all the 200 houses are newly built. But not all of them. There are five or six cottages, now uninhabited and uninhabitable, which were clearly standing at the time of the massacre.

Glencoe

Preston (1715)

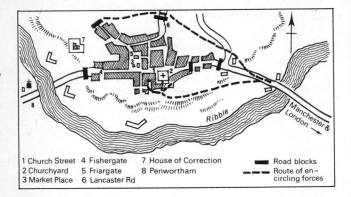

1 Church Street 4 Fishergate 7 House of Correction ▬ Road blocks
2 Churchyard   5 Friargate   8 Penwortham   ----- Route of en-
3 Market Place 6 Lancaster Rd   circling forces

The accession of William and Mary was accepted politically by the Scots, partly because Mary was pure Stuart and William quarter Stuart, and they were felt to be preferable to the deserter, but there were many Scotsmen who believed that a male Stuart should at least be the King of Scotland, if not of the United Kingdom.

Queen Anne, the last of the Stuart monarchs, died in 1714. By the Act of Settlement the son of James II, the Old Pretender, was absolutely excluded from the throne as he was a Roman Catholic, the nearest successor being the Hanoverian, George I. But he was a Protestant, unpopular and could speak no English. He was received in London and by the people, but in Scotland there at once arose a movement to recall young James from France to be Scotland's king.

The Earl of Mar, whose loyalty wavered between the Hanoverian king and the Jacobite pretender, was publicly snubbed by King George at a levee in London. Immediately he declared himself for young James and left by boat for

Scotland. Here he quickly gathered an army of several hundred Scotsmen, sending out recruiting parties into the Highlands. Soon he had so augmented his force that the whole of Scotland north of Edinburgh was in his hands.

After much manoeuvring in the Highlands Mar decided to invade England, although the Old Pretender had not yet left Paris. A portion of the newly raised rebel army under General Forster crossed the border at Carlisle, and marching over Shap passed through Penrith, Kendal and Lancaster. Here they stayed for three days, spending much time in arguing with the colonel of the local militia – the ancestor of the 5th (Territorial) battalion of the King's Own Royal Lancaster Regiment – as to the rights and wrongs of their invasion. The Lancastrians, finally bored with the discussions, marched off to Wigan, where they joined a force of regular English regiments under General Willis, bringing the total number to meet the Scots up to 3,000.

The rebels reached Preston first and immediately put the town into a state of defence by erecting barricades across the main streets. Thus Church Street was closed to the east, so blocking the only line of advance for the Hanoverian army from Wigan or across the Ribble bridge. Fishergate was similarly closed to access from the ford at Penwortham, while Lancaster Road and Friargate were blocked to prevent entry from the north. In each case the major barricade had a subsidiary farther out, as a delaying position. Many of the houses round all the barricades were loopholed for the musketeers, and the centre of Preston became a temporary fortress.

General Willis detached a mounted and a dismounted force, each of about 700 men, to cross the Ribble bridge, a mile to the south-east of the town, and thence march right round Preston. Here it was to demonstrate against the town from the north and to cut off a line of retreat to Scotland in case of a withdrawal. He then sent the Lancaster militiamen also to cross the bridge and, bearing left, advance uphill to the southern edge of the town, while a regular infantry regiment, the Cameronians, were to attack the eastern barricades across Church Street. It was almost a complete envelopment.

All went according to plan. The militia covered themselves with glory, capturing the houses round the churchyard. Then, moving farther west, they tried to assault the barricade in Fishergate, but were held. The Cameronians forced the outer barricade at the eastern end of Church Street and drove the defenders back to the main barricades near the parish church. Leaving the Cameronians and the militia to keep up pressure Willis then sent reinforcements round to the north to push the attack up Friargate. Gradually the perimeter of the defences shrank, and when darkness came the Scotsmen were entirely hemmed in. Many houses captured by Willis's men were set on fire and by the light of the flames there was considerable infiltration. When the fighting died down about midnight the rebels were in a tight circle round the market place, with their attackers strongly pressing them in Friargate from the north. Soon after midnight Colonel Cotton, on Willis's staff, bravely rode through the lines to the Mitre Inn in the market square, General Forster's headquarters, asking if they wished to surrender. A few hours' grace was demanded before a decision was given and Cotton returned to Willis. On his way through the barricade at the end of Church Street his orderly was killed by a sniper from a house overlooking the street, and in full view of many men of the Cameronians, who were resting. Such an action, always bitterly resented by the British soldier, did not improve relations between the two sides.

At dawn next day the rebels surrendered, the Cameronians supervising the disarmament. There can have been little kid-glove treatment. The Jacobite officers gave up their swords in the church, but the Scottish peers declined this humiliation and surrendered them in private at the Mitre.

The British forces lost 143 men killed, with 130 wounded, while the rebels lost only 42, but over 1,000 were taken prisoner.

Today it is difficult to pinpoint exactly the sites of the barricades, except the outlying one which the Cameronians first captured. Church Street is, of course, much wider today than in 1715, but it is probable that the barricade crossed the street from the modern Lamb Hotel to near the National Westminster Bank, while its inner partner was very close to the parish church. The barricade covering the Penwortham ford ran across the road near the present main-line railway under the road, or possibly a little nearer the town. The Mitre Inn has disappeared and the site is now occupied by Burton's, the tailors. All the streets round the market square, especially Church Street, Fishergate and Friargate, are on precisely the same sites as in 1715. The parish church was largely rebuilt in 1855 and is on the original foundations. The lower part of the tower is, however, the one existing in 1715. It dates from soon after the Conquest and saw much of the fighting. The slope of the hill up which the Lancaster militia first charged after crossing the Ribble bridge is much steeper than one might expect. The successful assault says much for the training, discipline and particularly the fitness of these irregulars.

Sheriffmuir (1715)

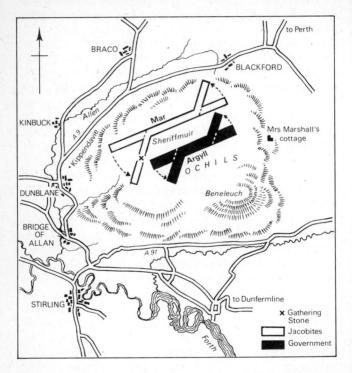

The Earl of Mar, leading the Jacobite rebellion of the '15, had dispatched a force of newly recruited rebels to invade England in November 1715. It had been halted at Preston, surrounded and forced to surrender.

Mar did not accompany it and, foolishly, having taken this initiative, dallied round Perth and Stirling with some 8,000 men undecided on how to seize power and secure the restoration of the Old Pretender. He was an appalling general and had to face the English government troops under the Duke of Argyll, a skilled leader trained by the great Duke of Marlborough. Argyll had only 3,800 men but they were trained, disciplined English or Lowland Regulars. The two armies met at Sheriffmuir on 13 November on the same day that the Jacobite rebels were defeated at Preston.

On 11 November Mar and his army marched south from Perth to seize the bridges over the Forth on either side of Stirling. They reached the village of Kinbuck, 2 miles north of Dunblane, where they spent the nights of 12 and 13 November in bitter cold, a few of the men finding a little shelter in the villagers' barns.

Argyll, hearing that Mar had marched south with his full force, left Stirling at once, putting an infantry soldier on the back of every cavalryman's horse. A forced march brought his 3,500 men on the evening of the 12th to Dunblane, where they found some shelter in the hamlets of Kippenrait, Stonehill, Newton and Dykedale, and in the fields of what is now the Hydropathic Establishment. Argyll himself slept in a building on the site of the present Dykedale Farm.

At 6 am on Sunday, 13 November, Mar's army was drawn up on the northern slopes of Sheriffmuir, to the south-east of the present Dunblane–Perth road through the farmstead of Lower Whitiestone.

When day broke the rebels could see the English regulars a mile away forming up near the 'Gathering Stone', a high-point on the western edge of the Muir, with cavalry out in front reconnoitring. (The Gathering Stone lies 600 yards north-west of the MacCrae memorial on the Dunblane–Millhill road and at the corner of Sheriffmuir Big Wood, but is not easily found.) Argyll's right was about point 1031, the highest point along the road, and some 900 yards north-east of the Sheriffmuir Inn, with his left near the Gathering Stone.

There were no trees there in 1715 and both armies could keep each other under observation.

Owing to Mar's hesitancy and, surprisingly, to Argyll's allowing the initiative to pass from him, no moves were made until 11 am, when Mar advanced on the right with most of his cavalry and half his infantry not against Argyll's left but, changing direction slightly to his left, diagonally across the front. Argyll immediately moved more infantry to his right to meet this threat.

In Mar's cavalry advance his infantry units became disorganized and lost cohesion in their uphill climb. He transferred the balance of his cavalry from his left flank to the right.

As Mar's right flank, now strengthened by the additional cavalry, considerably overlapped Argyll's now truncated left, the advance was successful and the English extreme left wing was cut to pieces. The action on this flank took only ten minutes and here Argyll's men were driven from the field. The Scotsmen, as usual, had discarded their shirts and muskets and had charged, semi-naked, to the battle with their fearsome swords, which they were so adept at wielding. The Old Pretender's cause looked promising.

But out on the other flank and higher up the Muir a similar action was being fought the other way round. Argyll had strengthened this wing on seeing the Highlanders' probable move across his front and he was now to enjoy the benefit of his tactics. Mar's left wing charged him in strength but now had no cavalry in support, leaving a vulnerable open flank. Seeing this, Argyll ordered his right wing cavalry, which included the Scots Greys, to ride round the rebels, now brought to a halt by the English infantry fire. The Scotsmen gave way and were pursued by the Greys right back over the river Allan to Kilbuck, near where they had spent the night.

Thus the tactical situation halfway through the battle was

surprisingly similar to that at Marston Moor 71 years before. In each case a considerable cavalry success on one flank was matched by a cavalry reverse on the other. As a result the whole battle line slewed round like a rugger-scrum, and had at half-time changed direction through 45°.

Apparently Argyll did not know for some time of the disaster to his left flank, being so occupied by his pursuit of Mar's left. But a large portion of Mar's infantry were still intact in the centre of the Muir, having now been joined by the victors of Argyll's defeated left. There were about 3,000 men here and the fact that Mar did not at once use this considerable force to cut off Argyll's successful right flank attack emphasizes his incapacity.

Argyll, well satisfied with his success on the right, returned to Sheriffmuir and as the light began to fail collected all the men whom he could find and moved back to Dunblane, where he was joined by the remnants of his shattered left wing. Crossing the river Allan he encamped at Hillside – very near the northern exit of the present railway tunnel on the Stirling–Perth line – his men understandably remaining under arms all night.

Mar was left in possession of the field, apparently the victor. But was he? He had lost his food wagons, which had been captured by Argyll's right-flank cavalry advance, his baggage horses had stampeded, his men were weary and cold and almost half of them believed they had been defeated, as indeed their left flank had been. After dark they too left the battlefield, Mar withdrawing to Ardock and thence to Perth.

Next morning, as soon as it was light, part of Argyll's army returned to the Muir to collect the wounded and with a bellicose spirit to renew the battle. But the field was deserted.

Argyll lost 470 officers and men killed and wounded, with 130 taken prisoner. Mar claimed to have lost only 60 men killed with 82 captured, but his figures are very suspect.

It may be said that neither side won a victory, yet Argyll's army, despite its tactical setbacks, had in the long run prevented the Jacobites from crossing the Forth and reaching Stirling and Edinburgh. The Old Pretender was further from recapturing his throne than before this inconclusive battle: a tactical stalemate, but a strategic victory.

Sheriffmuir has changed little since 1715. The large wood to the west of the Gathering Stone is rather smaller but the rest of the battlefield is still a wild, windswept moor of heather, peat and bog. This desolate spot is crossed by a good second-class road running just behind the crest on which the English formed up, and runs up from Dunblane and then down to Millhill. At a road junction about halfway between the Mac-Crae memorial and point 1031 is the Sheriffmuir Inn. Its owner, Mrs Marshall, lives there alone and frequently in the winter in her isolation will see no pedestrians, motorists or farmhands for several days on end. In her little bar two claymores are displayed, and a 1715 musket, much cleaned and restored, all picked up on the battlefield.

Prima facie the whole moor is ideal cavalry country with no natural obstacles to impede horsemen at a gallop. Conversely it is unsuited for infantry since it has no features to hold, defend, outflank or assault. Yet the ground is just the reverse. It is so heavy, the going so bad, the frequent little patches of bog so treacherous that formed bodies of horse could scarcely move above a trot. Equally, provided both flanks of a defending force are 'refused', it is difficult to manoeuvre a resolute infantry enemy out of his position. At all times an advancing enemy is in full view, there being no cover whatever, while the defending infantry are of course also entirely in full view.

The Gathering Stone, as well as being difficult to find, is

not very interesting. It is in fact two large boulders, and one small one, about 2 feet high and enclosed under a stout iron grille, lying isolated among a few trees. Were it not for the fact that Argyll's left flank rested here, the Stone would be of little interest. The view eastward along the English line to point 1031, and northward, is superb and well worth a good walk, but gumboots are advisable.

Prestonpans (1745)

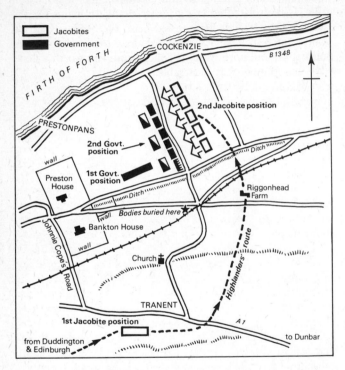

In the 30 years after the fiasco of the '15 little was heard of the Stuarts – or the succession. But early in 1745, after the defeat of the British army at Fontenoy, the unpopularity of George II, who had succeeded his non-English-speaking father, caused the exiles in Paris to believe the climate fair for another attempt on the Scottish throne. The Young Pretender, Bonnie Prince Charlie, son of the Old Pretender, landed on the west coast of Scotland to reclaim his father's inheritance. Here he gained the support of the great clans – the Camerons and the Macdonalds – and marched south.

He proclaimed his father as James VIII of Scotland. He then went on to Edinburgh where he installed himself in Holyrood House.

Prince Charles must have been fearful as to the outcome of his hazardous adventure. To march militarily forward, to try and seize the throne by force of arms, was foolhardy in the extreme. His men were only clansmen, primitively armed, unorganized, almost untrained, with no supplies, stores or transport, and lacking all discipline beyond patriotism. They were to meet the trained regulars of the English army, men who had fought at Dettingen and Fontenoy. He could not win. But he was a prince and soldiers always love a royal leader. He was young and good-looking. He was obviously an adventurer, another quality soldiers like, and he would, they thought, pick Scotland up and throw the hated English out of their country.

Charles stayed in Edinburgh for four days and there beat up volunteers to join his force. This affront to the sovereignty of England was taken very seriously in London, and to meet it General Cope, with four English regiments, the Royal Warwicks, the Essex, the Loyals and the Duke of Cornwall's Light Infantry, stationed in Aberdeen, was ordered to embark and sail to Dunbar. From there they were to march west, reoccupy Edinburgh and reassert the king's government.

Cope's army disembarked at Dunbar and, using the coast road, marched west, passing over the present golf course of Gullane and just missing that of Muirfield. He passed through Longniddry intending to reach Musselburgh.

On arrival at Seaton on the main road to Edinburgh, Cope heard that the prince was marching to Tranent. Cope took up a position near the village of Prestonpans facing south-west across the plain between the mansion of Preston Grange and Seaton House, 1½ miles apart. His back was to the sea half a mile behind him, while in front lay a deep ditch, stone dykes, a thick thorn hedge and a considerable bog, the whole covering a mile of frontage.

The prince had 2,500 men under his command. The men in his ranks were wild, strong, active, hearty men much helped by their appearance. The Highland kilt showed their muscular legs and knees, while their bushy uncombed hair and stern faces gave them a fierce and imposing demeanour. It cannot be denied that had they been clothed and groomed like average men or soldiers they would have seemed very ordinary, and their success against Cope's infantry would not have been so easy or widespread.

The Highlanders' armament was very sketchy. A goodly number had firearms but these were mostly old fowling-pieces, or defective muskets from the Edinburgh armoury where they had been sent for repair. In any case good as these muskets might have been, the eighteenth-century Highland soldier did not think much of firearms, new-fangled weapons that few of them understood. A few Highlanders still carried the broadsword but the great majority were swordsmen of great ability. A few of the men had no weapons at all at the beginning of the campaign. To overcome this deficiency they attached scythe-blades to the ends of wooden poles 7 or 8 feet long. These were difficult to wield but a terrible wound could result from the swinging blow landing on a limb of an opponent unable to avoid it: an arm or leg or head could easily be severed.

The Highlanders climbed the western edge of the high ground on which Tranent stood; from here they could see the English army drawn up on the plain below them. They saw its straight lines, its cohesion, its obvious discipline. During the afternoon the Highlanders became restive and clearly ready to charge down the slope at their enemy. Charles, too, was impatient of delay, anxious to join battle, but his staff advised caution.

Early in the evening Charles, riding round, fell in with a Mr Anderson, owner of a large house, out beyond the far left flank of Cope's position. Here he held a council of war with his second-in-command, Lord George Murray, another staff officer (the Earl of Home, an ancestor of Sir Alec Douglas-Home) and old Mr Anderson and his nephew Robert, both staunch Jacobites. The nephew told Murray that he knew of a causeway across the bog within a short distance of Cope's left flank and that its passage would be both safe and secret. Murray told Charles that it was a heaven-sent chance, advising an immediate move of the Highland army to the east. Charles agreed and at 3 am the entire army was standing to, ready to march down to the new-found crossing.

Cope moved his lines, now to face due east, and roughly along the road then running from Tranent north-west to the coast at the fishing village of Cockenzie. This road is still in use, on its 1745 site. One solitary old thorn tree stood alone just behind the English line.

The right of the line rested on the ditch running along its flank, and to cover it Cope posted his guns and the doubtful dragoons. Next came the Essex Regiment, the Royal War-wicks, the Loyals and then the DCLI. The left flank was covered by a small party of cavalry.

Charles ordered stand to for 3 am. Led by young Mr Anderson the Macdonalds, in the lead, were followed by the Camerons, the Stewarts and the Macgregors. Behind these came the clans who would, on turning left, form the reserve line: the Atholmen, Robertsons, MacLachlans and Grants.

A faint streak of dawn was showing as the Highland army marched north-east down the Tranent ridge, through the

farmyard of Riggon Head and then due north where young
Anderson led them on to the path which crossed firstly a
bridge over the main ditch and then the marsh.

By 5 am the leading Macdonald regiments had cleared
Seaton House, leaving it on the right with the leading unit
almost opposite Cope's left northern flank. A gap had opened
up in the column and Lord George Murray, seeing it, ordered
the Macdonalds to halt, face left and wait until the next units
had closed up, when they too would face left.

Cope had some 2,600 officers and men with six guns. All
were trained, with modern arms, organized and professional.
Prince Charles had 2,500 men, almost parity, but they lacked
the modern arms and military qualities that Cope's men
possessed. But these deficiencies were compensated for by
their patriotic fervour: 'Thrice is he armed that hath his
quarrel just.' The justice of Prince Charles's case is not for
discussion here. Suffice it to say that the Highlanders were in
no doubt on this point.

Charles, impatient to start, went over to the Macdonalds to
give final instructions. On his way back he met two Macdonald officers away from their regiments and shouted at
them to hurry. The left-hand regiments, Camerons, Stewarts
and Macgregors, heard the shouting and, supposing it to be
the order to advance, moved forward; in a few seconds the
whole of Prince Charles's army was advancing across the
400 yards to where Cope's line could now be seen. It presented
a formidable sight.

One English gun fired, its ball badly wounding a Cameron,
who shrieked in his agony. His cry was like a match to tinder
and the whole line of Highlanders broke into a charge, fiercely
shouting their Gaelic war cries.

The Stewarts of Appin reached the guns before more than
five rounds could be fired and the gunners were overwhelmed
in a wave of tartan. The doubtful dragoons lived up to their

reputation and, seeing the gunners defeated, rode off the field.

This disaster to the guns and the defection of the dragoons created a panic, which quickly spread to the regiments in the centre of the line.

The two left-hand English regiments, the Loyals and the DCLI, seeing the Royal Warwicks wavering on their right and then the menace of the 900 Macdonalds bearing down on them, broke up, dispersing in any direction away from the Macdonalds. Five hundred of Cope's total force were quickly killed, with another 1,400 taken prisoner. The losses of the Highlanders were trifling, 4 officers and 40 men were killed, while only 6 officers and 80 men were wounded.

The excited and exultant Highlanders ran through and round the fleeing groups of redcoats, cutting them down mercilessly with their claymores. Round the old thorn tree and right up to the wall of Preston Grange, almost a mile behind the front line, were groups of English corpses.

Today Prestonpans has much to show. The farm buildings and the farmyard of Riggon Head through which the High-landers moved in the night in their flank march are precisely on the foundations of those of 1745. The mud in the farmyard is the same mud that the Macdonalds trod!

The ditch and the bog protecting Cope's front and then when he faced east his right flank have largely been drained, but parts of the ditch still exist. A good road now runs north from Riggon Head across the main A1 on to Cockenzie, crossing a clearly seen length of the ditch by a good modern bridge. Two hundred yards to the west was the little wooden bridge, which has now disappeared, across which young Mr Anderson led Charles's army.

The battle of Prestonpans, *after Sir W. Allan*

The main field of the battle today is largely covered with a vast vegetable market garden, on very black heavy soil. Now as in 1745 there is not an inch of cover. The Highlanders' charge was over at least 400 yards, and the physical effort must have been considerable, while the cool ranks of the English regiments were apparently at a considerable advantage.

The western portion of the battlefield is now covered with an enormous power station up to whose boundary an extensive housing estate has crept. As a result Preston Grange has been engulfed, as well as the site of the thorn tree. However, when the foundations of the housing estate were being dug a number of bodies were exhumed. These were brought to a little triangular site on the main road some 500 yards away and there reinterred, the plot being consecrated. The old thorn tree had to be removed and is now in Edinburgh Museum, but a sturdy cutting was taken from it and replanted in the centre of the new burial ground, where it is now 4 feet high and seems to be well established.

Looking at the great open battlefield today, of which two-thirds is unchanged, it becomes increasingly difficult to account for the defeat of 2,600 trained, disciplined, experienced regulars by an almost similar number of untrained, ill-disciplined clansmen. Looking at the problem from every military, technical and tactical angle and weighing up all the qualities or their absence on each side, one is left with the only conclusion possible: numbers being equal, burning fanatical patriotism is more than a match for discipline and cold steel.

Falkirk (1746)

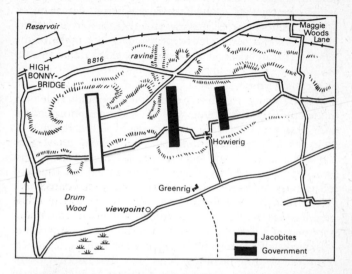

Early in 1746 Bonnie Prince Charlie and his army crossed back into Scotland from their foray into England. They had got as far as Derby but there discretion turned them back, and they reached the area round Stirling, mustering about 8,000 men. They were clearly still a menace to the English government, which feared that a large-scale French landing on the south coast of England might be made to embarrass the English while they were so busy in Scotland, or on Scottish soil to support Prince Charles and his Jacobites. Accordingly General Hawley collected an English army near Newcastle and marched to Edinburgh and thence to Linlithgow. Under his command were 12 famous regiments, of which details are given below.

Meanwhile the Jacobite army, bivouacked near Bannock-

burn, moved down to meet the Royalist army, on the high
ground, Falkirk Moor, south-west of Falkirk. Marching
across country they crossed the river Carron at Duniplace
Steps, 2 miles west of Falkirk, and then moved up on to
Falkirk Moor, a bare, windswept, boggy and rocky plateau.
The royal army was now in a temporary camp round Arnott
Hill just west of the town, with no outposts, scouts or any
protection whatsoever.

About 2 pm on 16 January a handful of peasants rode into
the royal camp with the news of the Jacobite moves and at
once near panic occurred. Regiments were ordered out at
once, the 13th Hussars leading, all units passing up Maggie
Woods Lane. The moor, less than a mile from the camp, was
occupied piecemeal. The King's Regiment led the infantry,
followed by the Border Regiment, Somerset Light Infantry,
the West Yorks, the Royal Scots and the East Lancs. On
reaching the top of the hill they halted, turned right and made
some sort of a line.

Immediately in front of the right of the line a steep-sided
ravine ran up from the low ground. The East Lancs skilfully
formed up behind it, keeping it as a protective ditch between
themselves and the enemy. At the other end of the line was a
large and impassable bog. A small farmhouse, Howierig, lay
in the centre of the second line of regiments, the Inniskilling
Fusiliers, Hampshires, Worcesters, King's Own, Wiltshires
and Buffs. On the left of the front infantry line and between
it and the bog the 11th, 13th and 14th Hussars were drawn
up.

At about 4 pm as the light was fading and the rain starting
General Hawley ordered the three cavalry regiments to charge
the Highlanders' right wing. They came in at a canter but the
Jacobites held their fire until the horsemen were within 20
yards. The volley was devastating and 80 Hussars were killed,
while most of those not wounded turned and fled.

The Macdonalds, as usual on the right of the line, could not be restrained and they charged forward into the left wing of the King's Regiment, causing some unsteadiness in that regiment and in the next two.

The heavy rain now prevented the stationary Highlanders in the front line from reloading their muskets after the repulse of the Hussar regiments. Throwing them away, as they were to do at Culloden three months later, they charged, sword in hand. The royal troops, blinded by the driving rain and sleet and already unsettled by the retreating cavalry and Macdonald charge, offered little resistance. The King's, the Border Regiment, the Somerset Light Infantry and the Royal Scots turned and ran. They blundered into the second line of regiments, three of which also collapsed, joining in the general *sauve qui peut*. However the King's Own, in the centre of the second line, the West Yorks and the East Lancs stood firm, forming a temporary brigade. They advanced up the hill to fire into the flank and rear of the pursuing clansmen, adding to their already extensive disorganization. This action by the new brigade caused the Highlanders to halt and then to retreat, many of them leaving the field.

The second line of the Jacobites now advanced, driving the new brigade slowly back down the hill and into the night. The Highlanders followed, disorganized, not knowing in which direction the royal army had retreated. They reached the camp occupied the previous night by the English but found it deserted. The English had marched away to Linlithgow.

As at Prestonpans the action was over in a very short time. It is estimated that only 25 minutes elapsed between the firing of the first shot and the eventual withdrawal of the King's Own, the last regiment to leave the field.

There is little doubt that the Jacobites' victory was partly due to the driving rain in the faces of the English as they confronted the advancing Highlanders. But it cannot be denied that their performance was deplorable. Their low morale declined still further and it is surprising that they could be collected next day and reformed at dawn.

To find the Muir the visitor must take the Falkirk–Slamannon road (B803). Six hundred yards after crossing over the main Glasgow–Edinburgh railway line, bear right for Cumbernauld. Two miles on is Greenrig Farm, with several cottages on both sides of the road. Another 200 yards farther on is the best viewpoint of the battlefield.

Out beyond Greenrig and to its left is Howierig Farm, where the King's Own and the West Yorks stood after the general collapse of the remainder of the line. On the other side of this road lies the bog. It is very evident today and shows clearly how the right and left flanks respectively of both armies were guarded. The upper end of the slight valley in which the bog lies is now being reclaimed for afforestation but still forms an almost impassable obstacle. The 11th and 13th Hussars charged across the ground, from right to left.

The visitor should drive on round Drum Wood, not existing in 1746, and down to Bonnybridge. There turn right immediately before entering the village and three-quarters of a mile farther on the road passes over the ravine behind which the East Lancs formed up. Although much hidden by low undergrowth and saplings, the ravine is seen today to be a very considerable obstacle, and while it is not impassable by active infantry must inevitably have so hindered an assault as to make it not worth while attempting. It was an effective barrier to cavalry, and even today a tank could not cross it.

Maggie Woods Lane is today a quiet, narrow little suburban road, on to which face dignified detached Georgian houses in their own grounds. The name of this little lane does not refer to a young lady. For many decades it indicated the way to the wood where magpies nested.

Culloden (1746)

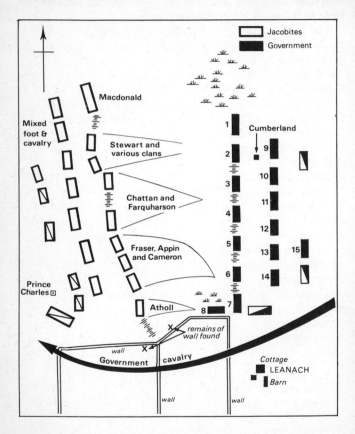

After Bonnie Prince Charlie's victory at Prestonpans, followed by his abortive invasion of England, he withdrew into Scotland, discredited but not defeated. Three months of bitter winter weather saw him and his utterly disorganized, always hungry army wandering in the Grampians. In April a force of 6,000 assembled at Inverness.

The English army under Cumberland marched north. On 14 April Prince Charles heard that the English had reached Nairn and were about to move on to Inverness. He marched out 6 miles eastward to Culloden Moor, bivouacking there for the night.

The morale of the Highlanders, already low from lack of food and an abortive night manoeuvre, sank even lower. By 6 am the whole force was back on Culloden Moor, no one thinking of anything but sleep and, if possible, food.

At about 9 am there was much free advice given to Charles by the leaders as to whether he should fall back on Inverness – or stay where he was. Advocates of each course again disagreed among themselves and argued with Charles. In addition there was much ill-feeling because the Camerons were not allowed to have the post of honour on the right, being replaced by the Athol Brigade.

Culloden Moor is a moor in every respect. It is still such a coarse piece of ground as to be quite unsuitable for the roughest agriculture. It is heavy going and in the lower levels bogs still exist. Between the final positions taken up by the opposing armies ran a slight hollow 50 yards wide containing heavy, muddy ground.

Key to numbers:

1	Somerset Light Infantry	8	King's
2	Royal Scots	9	Wiltshire
3	Border Regiment	10	Buffs
4	West Yorks	11	Worcesters
5	Scots Fusiliers	12	Northamptons
6	Hampshires	13	Lancashire Fusiliers
7	King's Own	14	K.O.S.B.
		15	Inniskilling Fusiliers

There were two large 'enclosures' whose drystone walling formed suitable cover for defending infantry. Surprisingly the Highlanders made little use of these walls, thereby showing the absence of professional military knowledge or 'eye for ground'. The right-hand enclosure, 'Culloden Park', had two cottages 200 yards out beyond its northern wall, Leanach Cottage.

At 5.30 am the royal army advanced towards Inverness. When it was 600 yards from the Highlanders' line all could see its greatly superior numbers and discipline. Its appearance did nothing to raise the spirits of the already tired Scotsmen.

The Macdonald clan now arrived on the battlefield and, without instructions, marched off to the left of the line, having found the right, which they too claimed, already occupied. Here they elbowed the then incumbent regiment off to its right and forced their way into the gap. Later in the day they refused to join in the general advance because they were not allowed to be on the right of the line. They remained sulking in their lines on the extreme left.

One of the striking features of the Battle of Culloden was the lack of a firm, dominating Jacobite commander who could make a plan, make decisions, issue orders. No one co-ordinated moves between the clans, no one allocated areas or reserves. Each clan fought almost as it pleased and largely according to the patriotism of its laird. Most were sensible enough to form a line and so prevent an English penetration, but there were no tactics.

When 500 yards away Cumberland ordered up his ten 3-pounder guns, and opened fire soon after 1 pm. The prince returned the fire at once, but Prince Charles's guns were ill-served, most being manned by scratch crews who, when counter-battery fire was directed on them, turned and fled.

The royal artillery fire was increased and irreparable damage was inflicted on the Highlanders, while Cumberland's men suffered virtually no casualties. They had only to wait for the enemy to advance against the regular infantry regiments and their musketry.

At about 2.30 pm the royal artillery fire changed from solid cannon-balls to grape-shot and the Highlanders in the front line became impatient at being kept stationary as 'cannon-fodder' and were restrained with difficulty from charging forward. An advance was eventually sanctioned but it was not co-ordinated and most clans moved forward irrespective of whether those on their right or left were moving or not. The centre of the line surged forward first, closely followed by several regiments on the right wing, but the still disgruntled Macdonalds on the left refused to obey.

In the centre was Clan Chattan, led by MacGillivray. The men were by now so exasperated at lack of food and the punishment they had received from the royal artillery that they raced towards the English lines, many of them throwing away their muskets because they hindered their speed. Half-way across the no man's land the clan suddenly swung to the right, masking many of the prince's best men in the right-wing regiments and thus preventing them from coming to grips with the enemy. Thanks to this swerve to the right the fire from the West Yorks and the Royal Scots Fusiliers caught the Highlanders in semi-enfilade and caused many casualties.

Because of the swerve the right-hand regiments became packed against the park wall, becoming so inextricably mixed that some 1,500 men continued forward in nothing more than mob-formation. By sheer force of numbers they got forward and found facing them the King's Own. This regiment, with fixed bayonets and in three ranks, waited until the enemy was within 30 yards, then opened fire. It was impossible to miss. Yet many Highlanders survived and, passing through, virtually split the regiment into two halves. The very weight of their charge carried them on, past the cannon in the area between the front and second line of infantry battalions, until they were brought to a halt by the fire from the Lancashire Fusiliers in the second line, which virtually exterminated them. The loss of men in the King's Own was very heavy, not only from the almost maddened Scotsmen, but from the fire of the regiments in the second line who brought the charge to a halt. The King's Own's loss from killed and wounded was 120 officers and men out of a total of 450, one-third of the total English casualties that day. Of the 1,500 Highlanders who started the charge 500 penetrated the King's Own. Very few of these 500 eventually survived, as many who fought their way back were caught by the fire of the flank guard, formed by the King's Regiment. Soon remnants of the great charge on the right came back and left the field – the Macdonalds following them.

Cumberland 'improved' his victory by letting his cavalry go into pursuit to round up the fleeing Highlanders and it is to the disgrace of these royalist horsemen that they killed, or rode down, many of the fugitives. Few prisoners were taken. Cumberland was in no hurry to follow his defeated enemy and ordered his regiments to 'dress their lines'. When all was ready he slowly advanced, leaving the King's Own and the Hampshires behind to lick their wounds. Several wounded Highlanders had taken refuge in Leanach Cottage, but a particularly savage royal captain with 50 men found them in the barn, locked the doors and set the building on fire. Thirty-two charred bodies were removed later.

Today the greater part of the battlefield is covered by a wood of pines and firs. There is, however, a strip about 150 yards by 300 largely untouched along the eastern side of the battle-field and there is much to be seen in it.

The little cluster of three farm buildings at Leanach Barn

is now reduced to one and the ruined foundations of another. The one remaining is virtually as it was in 1746, with little restoration. It stood just behind the King's flanking position and was occupied as a crofter's residence until 1912. It is now an attractive and romantic little museum. A few yards away are the foundations of the barn where the wounded Highlanders were found by the English. The murder of the 32 helpless soldiers inside was typical of the cruelty practised by the royal army after their victory. It has not been forgotten by the Scots.

In the no man's land between the two opposing armies, at its eastern end, lie the mass graves of many of the clans. Each has a rough-hewn, weather-worn stone at the outer end of each mound, about 3 feet high, with the name of the clan crudely carved upon it. Just in front of the King's Regiment's left flank is the mass grave of the English dead with a simple statement of the losses.

Leanach Cottage, now a museum

The exact positions of most regiments, English and Scots, are almost impossible to identify owing to the wood and undergrowth. An exception is the two left-hand English regiments, the King's Own being astride the modern Inverness–Nairn road, and the King's, whose positions were clear of the modern wood. They can be pinpointed very accurately to within 20 yards, but the position of the regiments on the right of the Hampshires on the King's Own right cannot be even conjectured after a few yards' walk into the wood.

All the military historians who have described the Battle of Culloden state that the stone walls on the battlefield, which played a considerable tactical role, have long since disappeared. The foundations of the wall against which the swerving Chattan Clan forced the Athol Highlanders and the Camerons can be found if carefully looked for. This wall is now the boundary of the big field out beyond the copse. It is 2 feet high and is largely covered with turf. Perhaps the most incontrovertible evidence of its being the original wall is that for about 100 yards it follows the precise line of the original wall shown on the sketch maps of 1746.

The little muddy dip between the lines of the two opposing armies and across which some of the Highlanders charged is still there. It is still muddy and enables the almost exact positions of the two left-hand regiments to be closely identified.

Direction-posts on the roads for some distance, indicating Culloden, are numerous and well sited. Two hours on the battlefield are sufficient to see everything in this small area.

Index